W9-AHM-563

**THE
NEW GLOBAL
ECONOMY
IN THE
INFORMATION AGE**

Martin Carnoy
Manuel Castells
Stephen S. Cohen
Fernando Henrique Cardoso

THE NEW GLOBAL ECONOMY IN THE INFORMATION AGE

REFLECTIONS ON OUR CHANGING WORLD

The Pennsylvania State University Press
University Park, Pennsylvania

Library of Congress Cataloging-in-Publication Data

The New global economy in the information age : reflections on our
  changing world / Martin Carnoy . . . [et al.].

p.   cm.
Includes bibliographical references and index.
ISBN 0-271-00909-8. — ISBN 0-271-00910-1 (pbk.)
1. Economic history—20th century.   2. World politics—20th
century.   3. Information society.   I. Carnoy, Martin.
HC59.N415   1993
330.9'04—dc20   92-33652
                                                         CIP

Second printing, 1996

Published by The Pennsylvania State University Press,
Barbara Building, Suite C, University Park, PA 16802-1003

It is the policy of The Pennsylvania State University Press to use acid-free paper for
the first printing of all clothbound books. Publications on uncoated stock satisfy the
minimum requirements of American National Standard for Information Sciences—
Permanence of Paper for Printed Library Materials, ANSI Z39.48–1984.

Published and distributed in paperback outside North America by
THE MACMILLAN PRESS LTD
Houndmills, Basingstoke, Hampshire RG21 2XS and London
Companies and representatives throughout the world

ISBN 0-333-59489-4

A catalogue record for this book is available from the British Library.

Contents

1

Introduction

The world economy has changed profoundly over the past three decades, and with those changes have come new political strategies for national development. Revolutionary transformations in the demand for goods and in the way they are produced have affected long-term national growth possibilities, how governments relate to their national economies, and how national economies relate to each other. The world economy is becoming more competitive, more global, and increasingly dominated by information and communications technology.

Nation-states still have a crucial role in influencing the course of their economic development. They also have a range of policy choices framed by political forces. This is evidenced by the variation in macroeconomic and social policies even among highly industrialized Western capitalist nations. But the "informatization" of the world economy changes the conditions and possibilities for national policies. It means the informatization of societies and politics. Economic globalization means the globalization of local social movements. Local becomes global, and global becomes local.

Previous political strategies, arrangements, and structures, organized around assembly-line industrialization economies, are as inefficient and obsolete as their economic base. The first political casualty of the information age is the communist state system, based on a 1920s-model hierarchical industrial organization and incapable of incorporating new, flexible management or rapidly changing technology. The inflexible communist state and the inflexible production system were so tied to one another that they collapsed together under the stress of world informatization. Capitalist states—even in their more adaptable democratic forms—are not immune to a less extreme but similarly radical transformation. Their politics are also intertwined with their production systems. Even multinational firms are rooted in national politics and national political choices, and they influence both. When capitalist states are inflexible, inefficient, and obsolete, they drag down their economies; when production systems have difficulty changing, they drag down their states.

This book is about such political economics and about the choices confronting nation-states. The following four chapters outline the new economic context in which nation-states operate, the main issues confronting them, and how the politics of national development should change in the post–Cold War information age. Each chapter is written from an *international* perspective because the economic *and* the political problems are global in nature. They are already being confronted on a global as well as a national scale.

Other writers have addressed these changes. The growth and concentration of large multinational enterprises, their dominance in the international economy, and their alleged "a-nationalistic" character has convinced some that the main function of the nation-state in the new world economy is to educate its citizens for participation in the world labor market. In this "economic globalization" view, nationalism and national wealth are embodied in the economic value of a nation's labor. Not only are multinational companies disconnected from their national origins, but national politics—even in the highly industrialized countries—are necessarily influenced by the needs and movements of international capital. Says Robert Reich:

> What is the role of a nation within the emerging global economy, in which borders are seeking to exist? My answer has, I hope, been

clear. Rather than increase the profitability of corporations flying its flag, or enlarge the worldwide holdings of its citizens, a nation's economic role is to improve its citizens' standard of living by enhancing the value of what they contribute to the world economy.[1]

National politics in such a view is subordinated to economics. The nation-state functions mainly as a supplier of human capital to complement multinational investments in machines and technology. It does not help define the character of multinational companies as social and political actors. Such definition comes from the "invisible hand" of a changing global economy. Neither does international politics have much impact on the global economy, particularly with respect to which nations get to participate and how.

Reich and others, such as Michael Porter, also argue that the nation-state can enhance the profitability of capital and labor at home by creating a good "environment" for investment in the local economy and for local economic development.[2] In combination with dynamic local firms, foreign investors drawn to this favorable environment improve the productive capacity of a region or nation. In the new world economic context, human capital and the favorable conditions for its development are crucial, but so are other factors: developmentalist, well-organized state interventions to promote local capital formation and innovation, for example.

We agree with this view but go beyond it. We are convinced that multinational enterprises are a product of their national origins and still depend on their home bases for economic strength. We are also convinced that there is a wide range of nation-state activity enhancing local economic development that goes beyond developing human resources for international distribution. We agree that no country is untouched by the economic revolution of the past two decades and that, like every revolution, it has created new winners and losers. Earlier than others, the winners understand the contours of the change. They adapt to it and even exploit it when the particular character and resources of their societies enable them to do so. The losers are locked into widely varying patterns of economic, social, and political behavior that are incongruent or simply not very harmonious with the kinds of action required in the new conditions.

1. Robert Reich, *The Work of Nations* (New York: Vintage, 1992), p. 301.
2. Michael Porter, *The Comparative Advantage of Nations* (New York: The Free Press, 1990).

Further, we view politics as key to the action that nation-states take to enhance their economies. Politics can and does go beyond creating an environment for capital accumulation. There is an inherent tension between democratic visions of society and the vision held up by national or multinational enterprises.[3] The democratic nation-state has historically had to develop institutions and pursue policies which reflect that democratic vision at the same time that it tries to create a suitable environment for capital accumulation.[4] In the information age, the democratic vision intensifies worldwide, putting increased pressure on local states to deal with new kinds of social movements while trying to adjust to the new needs of a changing global economy. At the same time, the efficient, flexible nation-state in the information age shapes the way domestic and foreign business enterprises interact with the national society, and it does so successfully through public policies that reflect information-influenced political demands.

Moreover, politics transcends national boundaries. In a global environment that is becoming more intensely global, it is not only economics that becomes more internationalized. So does politics.[5] National governments attempt to shape the nature of the international economy, often for ideological reasons as much as for practical economic gain. More recently, national populations have been rejecting "nation"-states, moving both outward and inward. If nation-states cannot be converted into more flexible, efficient forms, some social movements may push for transferals of power to other states or transnational entities. Northern Italians are

3. Fred Bloch, in *Postindustrial Possibilities* (Berkeley and Los Angeles: University of California Press, 1990), raises a number of important points around the issue of defining national economic progress in the post-assembly-line era. Social demands for environmental quality, improved working life, and improved home life all have implications for how economic progress is defined in the information age. They also have implications for economic productivity.

4. See Samuel Bowles and Herbert Gintis, *Capitalism and Democracy* (New York: Basic Books, 1986). In Robert Reich's model, the tension is reduced when the nation-state converts everyone into "symbolic analysts" through education. Then everyone becomes part of the information economy. This makes sense, but there are many fewer information jobs than there are workers, even in the United States.

5. The Maastricht Treaty, signed in 1991, is a good example of an attempt to institutionalize a transnational state as part of regionalized economic arrangements. The European Economic Community (EEC) nations signing the Treaty agreed to a single European currency and to Community-determined national macroeconomic policies by the end of the decade. Although the Treaty has to be ratified by referendum in each of the Community's member nations, and although Denmark's referendum failed in 1992, it is likely that some compromise will be made to salvage the essence of the agreement. If it is, the EEC will become a regional economy, with economic policy made in the EEC's administrative capital, Brussels.

much more anxious to join a European state than Neapolitans, who have prospered from the inefficiency of Italian state apparatuses. The population of the German Democratic Republic voted overwhelmingly to join the West as a reaction not only against the oppressiveness of its communist regime, but because they had greater faith in West German bureaucrats than in East German democrats to deliver the goods. In the contrary direction, subnational movements in Yugoslavia, the former Soviet Union, and Czechoslovakia are moving inward into what are supposed to be more coherent, flexible units reflecting local needs.

The new world economy cannot be separated easily from the new world society, and politics is the cement that binds the two. In the chapters that follow, we develop this theme by analyzing the nature of the new world economy, the changing face of multinational enterprises, national strategies of highly developed economies, and the changing conflict between North and South. We conclude that the profound economic changes of the past generation imply new kinds of political strategies and political arrangements. Those which work, we argue, will have to be consistent with the profound transformation in the way the world collects, processes, and communicates information. That means more inclusion, more democracy, and, ironically, more political influence over the shape of markets and social outcomes by well-organized, efficient states.

THE NEW WORLD INFORMATION ECONOMY

In the changed world economy, the sources of higher productivity are increasingly dependent on knowledge and information applied to production, and this knowledge and information is increasingly science-based. Production in the advanced capitalist societies shifts from material goods to information-processing activities, fundamentally changing the structure of these societies to favor economic activities that focus on symbol manipulation in the organization of production and in the enhancement of productivity.

The organization of production and of economic activity in general changes from standardized mass production to flexible customized production, and from vertically integrated large-scale organizations to vertical disintegration and horizontal networks between economic units. The new economy is global. Investment, production, management, markets, labor, information, and technology are organized across national boundaries. What is new is not so much that international trade is an important part of each nation's economy, but that national economies now work as units at the world level in real time. This gives multinational firms a tremendous advantage, for they already have the knowledge required to produce and market goods and services internationally. These large corporations have also been able to decentralize, both internally and in their relationship to networks of smaller, supplier firms.

Such economic and organizational transformations are taking place in the midst of one of the most significant technological revolutions in human history. Its core is information technology—informatics, microelectronics, and telecommunications—surrounded by and aiding scientific discoveries in other fields, such as biotechnology, new materials, lasers, and renewable energy. All this has been stimulated by economic and organizational transformations on a global scale; and, simultaneously, the new information technology is indispensable for such transformations.

The revolution in information technology has combined with organizational changes at the global level to produce a "new world information economy." Within the emerging global system, the structure and logic of the information economy defines a new international division of labor. That division is based less on the location of natural resources, cheap and abundant labor, or even capital stock and more on the capacity to create new knowledge and to apply it rapidly, via information processing and telecommunications, to a wide range of human activities in ever-broadening space and time.

How does the new division of labor play out in the world arena? In his analysis of the new world information economy, Manuel Castells develops the following argument. Both the demand for new products and the capacity to create and produce them are still concentrated in the major industrial powers. Yet, there is a difference: U.S. hegemony, developed in a period when closeness to large markets and economies of scale in manufacturing dominated comparative advantage, has declined as other national economies—notably Japan and, at the core of the European Economic Community, West Germany—exploited their scientific knowledge and management skill to compete successfully under conditions of more flexible, export-oriented manufacturing. As a result, U.S. hegemony has been replaced by a multipolar system of economic power that benefits several dominant countries and regions.

Further, a second tier of efficient producers of electronic goods and

high-technology hardware has sprung up in Asia—again, built on a base
of high-level technological and management skills and on a commitment
by the state to the promotion and application of those skills. Economies
such as those of South Korea, Taiwan, Hong Kong, and Singapore have
made astounding gains since the early 1960s. They, along with Japan,
constitute the most dynamic pole of the new world economy.

At the other end of the spectrum, much of Latin America and Africa
has suffered because of changes in the world economy. The heavy
borrowing that these national economies undertook to overcome their
structural problems in the 1970s became their huge debt burden of the
1980s. It rang the death knell of their traditional import-substitution
process. And this financial crisis occurred at the very moment when large
investments were needed for new imported technology, for new types of
local production, for industrial reorganization, and for more schooling,
worker training, and research. Effectively, debt burdens prevented such
investments, leaving many economies that otherwise might have partici-
pated in the sort of transformation occurring in Asia—e.g., Brazil, Mexico,
Argentina, Nigeria, Venezuela—far behind in the process of change, and
thrusting others—e.g., low-income, predominantly agricultural economies of Africa, Asia, and Latin America, even further outside the world
development process than in the past.

As a result, the concept of the Third World as such has disappeared.
What used to be known as Third World economies have now been
redefined according to their ability to produce goods and services related
to information. They fall into four groups: 1) the clear winners in the
new international division of labor—the rapidly growing, newly industrializing countries in Asia; 2) the potential winners, such as Mexico (as part
of a North American free-trade area) and Brazil; 3) the large continental
economies of India and China which, primarily because of their potentially
huge markets and large stock of highly skilled human capital, are on their
way to integration into the new world economy; and 4) the clear losers—
the Fourth World of marginal rural economies and sprawling urban
peripheries.

The future of the potential winners and the large continental economies
depends largely on how they transform their economic and educational
organizations and how they relate their existing but rudimentary R&D to
production. What happens in the Fourth World, on the other hand, is
more a function of creating totally new institutions and new bases of
economic and social integration. Whether the currently dominant trickle-

down, free-enterprise ideology promulgated by the major international agencies will push the Fourth World in that direction (or leave it worse off in the future) remains to be seen. We may likewise wonder what effect the collapse of communism and the transformation of the command economies of Eastern Europe and the former Soviet Union will have on the information economy. The incorporation of these regions—with their vast stock of technical and industrial capacity but with seriously undeveloped communications, information, and economic infrastructure—poses enormous problems but promises great potential. Indeed, the economic and political disintegration of the former Soviet Union and the inability of the industrial core to mobilize sufficient capital to prevent it may well produce the new world economy's first real crisis. On the other hand, should the vast markets and trained labor forces of the East turn the corner, their positive impact on the advanced economies and the newly industrialized countries could be just as profound.

MULTINATIONAL CORPORATIONS AND THE NATION-STATE

Multinational corporations and nation-states are key actors in shaping the direction of the information economy. They also are crucial to each national economy's position in the new international division of labor. Although these actors were important to the progress of national economies before all the changes of the past generation, their roles have changed.

The shift to information and its application to material production in a global context as the principal source of the wealth of nations has made the skills imbedded in multinational firms even more fundamental to a national economy's success. Their ability to process and use information on an international scale and their very size, implying a capacity for mobilizing investment capital and, more important, for conducting research and development on new products and applications, make them powerful players in a world that increasingly values such capacities. Small and medium-size firms are often more flexible, more efficient producers, or quicker to develop new products. But very little of the world's total R&D is done in such firms, and, ultimately, the most successful ones necessarily become multinationals.

In Chapter 3, Martin Carnoy shows that over the past fifteen years the most rapid growth among large multinational enterprises (MNEs) has been in electronics and computers. Oil companies, once the largest and fastest-growing MNEs, have declined steadily in the 1980s, although the 1990s may prove to be much more favorable. The shift has not only been from oil to high tech. Japanese companies have grown much more rapidly than U.S. and European MNEs, reflecting Japan's earlier and better understanding of the information economy.

The fact that some countries' MNEs have increased their output and worldwide influence so much more rapidly than others, especially the U.S. MNEs, suggests that earlier conceptions of multinational enterprises as "transnationals," above and beyond their nation-state home base, are incorrect. The nation-state's policies have a profound influence on the capacity of its MNEs to expand, for two reasons: 1) for most MNEs the home market is still crucial to the overall capital-accumulation process— national macroeconomic policies are important for home-market development; and 2) most MNEs' research-and-development capability is linked to home-base, nation-state R&D policies, high-skill human capital development policies, and telecommunications policies.

The nation-state is therefore still a crucial actor in the new world economy. But, Carnoy suggests, its role has changed. First, it has less leeway to focus its policies on developing national markets. For most countries, just to give investors access to the consumers and producers of that country is not enough to attract capital. Second, the nation-state now has to be much more concerned than in the past about acquiring or developing information technology that transforms its productive capacity: such technology involves management skills, telecommunications, computer hardware and software, and the high-level engineering skills required to adapt and supervise the use of the new technology. Even if the hardware portion of such technology is imported, it is crucial that the software (including management) be localized. That means that government policies concerning education, R&D, and incentives for adopting and developing new technologies must be much more aggressive than in the days of Henry Ford.

And because good management and organization for technology adoption and development requires public policies that are more coherent than simple resource exploitation or even assembly-line production, nation-states themselves need to be better managed, clearer in their objectives, and more in tune with world information systems than in the past.

What about the relationship between nation-states and multinational enterprises? With so many of the skills and hardware basic to participation in the information economy belonging to MNEs, one of the most important new roles of the nation-state is bargaining with these technology carriers in order to transfer knowledge into the local economy. This is not an easy task. MNEs are not eager to transfer their highest-return skills to others, and most nation-states have little bargaining power. But this is a two-way street. Nation-states that are able to develop coherent *general* knowledge-acquisition strategies are more likely to be ready to learn "on the job" from MNEs, should they locate locally. Too, most MNEs find it more advantageous economically to spread skills around in those nation-state environments where there are aggressive learning policies. Nation-states that have coherent national policies on the acquisition of information technology are also more likely to know what to bargain for and what their bargaining chips are.

NATIONAL STRATEGIES IN THE NEW WORLD ECONOMY

The nation-state also has a continued role as a political unit defining the economic space in which MNEs and domestic firms operate, and a say in how that definition changes on the basis of changing relations among nation-states. When the United States was in a hegemonic economic and military position, it did not regard the development of technological skills and competitive productive capacity in other militarily friendly countries as economically threatening. Indeed, others states' economic development was viewed almost entirely in its relationship to the political and military competition with the Soviet Union. Similarly, other nation-states were able to develop their own productive capabilities and knowledge systems within this same context, obtaining know-how from the United States in exchange for political loyalty.

The U.S. response to this gradual shift to a multipolar world and its lessons for Europe are discussed by Stephen Cohen in Chapter 4. Cohen shows that the Reagan administration's "solution" to increased international competition and informatization was to deregulate such critical sectors as telecommunications, air transport, and financial services, to break unions and lower real wages, to decrease federal tax rates, and to redistribute income to the top 1 percent of income earners. The idea was to make U.S. industry more competitive through cheaper labor and to legitimize such action politically through lower tax rates. There has also been a gradual shift in the United States toward protecting know-how for economic reasons and toward pushing hard for access of U.S. producers to markets (both for investment and sales) and against protectionist and import-substitution policies. At the same time, the U.S. government has made it much easier for highly skilled foreigners to immigrate and work in the United States and is attempting, somewhat late in the game, to develop a free-trade area (Canada, Mexico, and the United States) that would rival the European Economic Community in size but that would have the advantage of cheap energy, cheap labor, and, potentially, a rapidly growing market (Mexico) for high-technology goods produced within the free-trade area. Again, the emphasis is on cheap inputs, not higher productivity.

The United States has also put more emphasis on the export of military technology, where it still has a vast comparative advantage and increasingly so for economic rather than military reasons. Even the Gulf War, for all the righteous posturing by the advanced states regarding Saddam Hussein, was fought to keep petroleum prices down (i.e., for domestic economic reasons) and as a way of testing and displaying U.S. military technological superiority.

Whatever the economic arguments for such a strategy, it is a profoundly ideological one—couched in free-enterprise and Cold War rhetoric—and, Cohen argues, one that has not worked. The failure of this particular response to the new conditions of the information age provides important clues to what does work, and what works, the argument continues, is an emphasis on production and productivity that in turn requires intelligent and equitable social policies—in other words, a national and regional policy that is very different from that which the United States undertook in the 1980s.

With the demise of the Soviet Union, the last reason for a military-political basis to the postwar world economic system falls by the wayside. The United States, in Cohen's terms, could be the big loser from this change. More than any other advanced capitalist country, it has based its economic strategies during the information revolution on military technology and military competition. The institutions of the U.S. nation-state are organized around the underlying premises of Cold War thinking. Yet, should the United States recognize the errors of the past two decades and

adjust quickly to the new situation, it has the most to gain. No other
country besides the republics of the former Soviet Union can shift
anywhere near the quantity of R&D resources from military to commercial ends.

A NEW DEPENDENCY OR A NEW HISTORY?

The impact of the new world economy has been just as great on North-
South relations as on North-North. For one thing, as Manuel Castells
suggests, some parts of the South are becoming increasingly irrelevant
and marginal to the world economy. In other parts, the possibilities for
information-based development are there, but a totally different set of
new policies is required. These policies would have to be based on the
development of human productive potential. In the closing chapter, Fernando Henrique Cardoso makes this case and goes a step farther.

Cardoso argues that, in the South as a whole, changing dependency
relations require a change in the character of the society as a whole—not
just the pursuit of autonomy-oriented economic policies, as in the past,
not just an investment in human skills. In much of the South, to bring
innovation into the heart of the economy means democratizing society
and reconstructing the state, much as such changes were necessary in the
former Soviet Union and its client states in Eastern Europe. Paradoxically,
in a new world economy where technique seems to generate control of
everything, this same technique presupposes political freedom and a
coherent national political project. In the face of the challenge of economic
modernization, the political conditions for progress are inherently tied to
the transformation of the state, not only to economic markets.

At the same time, argues Cardoso, dependency relations will not change
and much of the South (and East) will not be incorporated into the new
world economy unless its problems are incorporated into the "global
problem." Politics must be globalized and extended to include the have-
nots and the illiterates—those without the new resources required to
participate in the information revolution—and this will not occur unless
politics North and South become "inclusive" at the national and international level. Inclusive politics are needed to overcome the new and
intensifying inequalities of information-producing capacity. At the same
time, by pursuing more inclusive politics, both North and South have the

best chance to fully develop the possibilities inherent in the information revolution.

Cardoso's chapter suggests something more. The collapse of communism in the information age signals not the "end of history"[6] but a new phase of conflict over the relationship between politics and economics. In the new phase, communist regimes are only the first victim in a series of clashes around the inability of old-style, bureaucratic politics to cope with the requirements of new economic organizations and new technologies. Increased democracy at the national and subnational levels will soon confront capitalist states—*including what Fukuyama calls liberal democratic states*—unable to navigate the waters of changing economic conditions and social demands. The end of history in this formulation is hardly the U.S. "liberal economics" model of the 1980s, progressively pauperizing the have-nots of its own nation and of the world. More realistically, new democratic political forms will emerge from a process that makes the information age as politically turbulent as the Renaissance or the age of industrial capitalism.

6. Francis Fukuyama, *The End of History and the Last Man* (New York: The Free Press, 1992).

2

Manuel Castells

The Informational Economy and the New International Division of Labor

THE INFORMATIONAL ECONOMY

We live in a new economy, gradually formed over the past half century and characterized by five fundamental features which are systemically interrelated. The first such feature is that sources of productivity—and therefore of economic growth in real terms—are increasingly dependent upon the application of science and technology, as well as upon the quality of information and management, in the processes of production, consumption, distribution, and trade. The pathbreaking work of Robert Solow in 1957,[1] followed by the aggregate-production-function studies on the sources of economic productivity by Denison, Malinvaud, Jorgenson, and Kendrick, among others,[2] has shown that advanced economies increased their productivity not so much as a result of the amount of capital or labor

1. Robert Solow, "Technical Change and the Aggregate Production Function," *Review of Economics and Statistics* 39 (1957): 312–20.

2. For a thorough discussion of the literature on the question of productivity sources, see Richard R. Nelson, "Research of Productivity Growth and Productivity Differences: Dead Ends and New Departures," *Journal of Economic Literature* 19 (September 1981): 1029–64.

added to the production process, as was the case in the early stages of industrialization, but as the outcome of a more efficient combination of the factors of production. Although econometric equations are obscure in identifying the precise sources of the new productivity pattern, the "statistical residual" found to be critical in the new production function has often been assimilated to the new inputs represented by the deeper penetration of science, technology, labor skills, and managerial know-how in the production process.[3]

A similar finding was reported on the evolution of the Soviet economy by Abel Aganbegyan, Gorbachev's first economic adviser. According to Aganbegyan's calculations, the Soviet economy grew at a robust rate until 1971, or as long as the state could rely on purely quantitative expansion by injecting more capital and labor and by pumping more and more natural resources into a rather primitive industrial structure. Once the Soviet economy became more complex, as a result of industrialization, it needed to introduce more sophisticated know-how into the production process in order to sustain growth. Because of the difficulty of developing and applying science and technology within a command economy, growth rates plummeted from 1971 onward, until reaching zero growth in the mid-1980s,[4] thus prompting the need for *perestroika* and precipitating the demise of Soviet communism.

Thus, it seems that the increasingly important role of applied knowledge and information is a characteristic of advanced economic systems, transcending the historical characteristics of their modes of production. It would also seem that the salient role of knowledge and technology is not exclusive to the late twentieth-century economy, nor has this economy resulted simply from a sudden change of production techniques. We are observing in fact a secular trend. Knowledge has always been important in organizing and fostering economic growth.[5] But the greater the complexity and productivity of an economy, the greater its informational component and the greater the role played by new knowledge and new

3. See Christian Sautter, "L'Efficacité et la rentabilité de l'économie française de 1954 à 1974," *Economie et Statistique* 68 (1976); Edward Denison, *Trends in American Economic Growth 1929–1982* (Washington, D.C.: Brookings, 1985).

4. Abel Aganbegyan, *The Economic Challenge of Perestroika* (Bloomington: Indiana University Press, 1988), pp. 10–11.

5. See Nathan Rosenberg and L. E. Birdzell, *How the West Grew Rich: The Economic Transformation of the Industrial World* (New York: Basic Books, 1986).

applications of knowledge (as compared with the mere addition of such production factors as capital or labor) in the growth of productivity.[6]

The second feature of the new world economy—and another secular trend that has accelerated in recent years—is the shift, in advanced capitalist societies, from material production to information-processing activities, both in terms of proportion of GNP and in the proportion of the population employed in such activities.[7] This seems to be a more fundamental change than the one proposed by the notion of the transition from industry to services, for today's "service sector" is so diverse that it becomes a residual category, mixing fundamentally different activities (from computer-software writing to cleaning floors) to the point that any analysis of economic structure must now start with a typological differentiation of the so-called service activities.[8] Furthermore, as Cohen and Zysman have forcefully argued,[9] there is a systemic linkage between manufacturing and the service sector, so that many such activities are in fact an integral part of the industrial production process.

Thus, the real transformation of the economic structure of advanced societies is the emergence of what Marc Porat in his seminal 1977 study labeled "the information economy," wherein an ever-growing role is played by the manipulation of symbols in the organization of production and in the enhancement of productivity.[10] In 1990, 47.4 percent of the employed population in the United States, 45.8 percent in the United Kingdom, 45.1 percent in France, and 40.0 percent in West Germany were engaged in information-processing activities, whether in the production of goods or in the provision of services,[11] and the proportion continues to rise over time.[12] Moreover, the quality of the information and one's efficiency

6. Jerome A. Mark and William H. Waldorf, "Multifactor Productivity: A New BLS Measure," in *Monthly Labor Review* 106 (December 1983): 3–15.

7. Tom Stonier, *The Wealth of Information: A Profile of the Postindustrial Economy* (London: Thames Methuen, 1983).

8. See Pascal Petit, *Slow Growth and the Service Economy* (London: Pinter, 1986).

9. Stephen S. Cohen and John Zysman, *Manufacturing Matters: The Myth of the Postindustrial Economy* (New York: Basic Books, 1987).

10. See Marc Porat, *The Information Economy: Definition and Measurement*, Special Publication 77-12(1) (Washington, D.C.: U.S. Department of Commerce, Office of Telecommunications, 1977).

11. Research in progress: data elaborated by Manuel Castells and Yuko Aoyama, University of California–Berkeley, 1992.

12. See Mark Hepworth, *Geography of the Information Economy* (London: Belhaven Press, 1989).

in acquiring and processing it now constitute the strategic factor in both competitiveness and productivity for firms, regions, and countries.[13]

Along with the fundamental changes taking place in the production process itself is a third feature of the new economy: a profound transformation in the *organization* of production and of economic activity in general. This change can be described as a shift from standardized mass production to flexible customized production and from vertically integrated, large-scale organizations to vertical disintegration and horizontal networks between economic units.[14] This trend has sometimes been assimilated to the dynamic role played by small and medium-size businesses (expressions of the new flexibility) in opposition to bureaucratized large corporations, as in the formulation of Piore and Sabel,[15] and has been discussed in the context of the so-called Third Italy Model of industrial development.[16] The organizational transformation of the economy, however, goes beyond the size of the firm and does not contradict the fundamental trend toward the concentration of economic power in a few major conglomerates. While it is true that small businesses have shown great resilience, becoming dynamic units in an advanced economy, the organizational pattern of decentralization and flexibility is also characteristic of large corporations, both in their internal structure and in their relationship to a network of ancillary firms, as is illustrated by the "just in time" supply technique introduced by the large Japanese automobile firms. Thus, the matter at hand is not so much the decline of the large corporation (still the dominant agent of the world economy) as it is the organizational transformation of all economic activity, emphasizing flexibility and adaptability in response to a changing, diversified market.

Fourth, the new economy is a global economy, in which capital, production, management, markets, labor, information, and technology are organized across national boundaries. Although nation-states are still fundamental realities to be reckoned with in thinking about economic

13. See Bruce R. Guile and Harvey Brooks (eds.), *Technology and Global Industry: Companies and Nations in the World Economy* (Washington, D.C.: National Academy Press, 1987).

14. See Robert Boyer, *Technical Change and the Theory of Regulation* (Paris: CEPREMAP, 1987).

15. Michael Piore and Charles Sabel, *The Second Industrial Divide* (New York: Basic Books, 1984).

16. See Vittorio Capecchi, "The Informal Economy and the Development of Flexible Specialization in Emilia-Romagna," in A. Portes, M. Castells, and L. Benton (eds.), *The Informal Economy: Studies in Advanced and Less Developed Countries* (Baltimore: Johns Hopkins University Press, 1989).

structures and processes, what is significant is that the unit of economic accounting, as well as the frame of reference for economic strategies, can no longer be the national economy. Competition is played out globally,[17] not only by the multinational corporations, but also by small and medium-size enterprises that connect directly or indirectly to the world market through their linkages in the networks that relate them to the large firms.[18] What is new, then, is not that international trade is an important component of the economy (in this sense, we can speak of a world economy since the seventeenth century), but that the national economy now works as a unit at the world level in real time. In this sense, we are not only seeing a process of internationalization of the economy, but a process of globalization—that is, the interpenetration of economic activities and national economies at the global level. The coming integration into the world economy of Eastern Europe, the former Soviet Union, and China—probably over the course of the next decade—will complete this process of globalization which, while not ignoring national boundaries, simply includes national characteristics as important features within a unified, global system.

Finally, these economic and organizational transformations in the world economy take place (and not by accident) in the midst of one of the most significant technological revolutions of human history.[19] The core of that revolution is in information technologies (microelectronics, informatics, and telecommunications) around which a constellation of major scientific discoveries and applications (in biotechnology, new materials, lasers, renewable energy, etc.) is transforming the material basis of our world in fewer than twenty years. This technological revolution has been stimulated in its applications by a demand generated by the economic and organizational transformations discussed above. In turn, the new technologies constitute the indispensable material base for such transformations.[20] Thus, the enhancement of telecommunications has created the material infrastructure needed for the formation of a global economy,[21] in a

17. See A. Michael Spence and Heather A. Hazard (eds.), *International Competitiveness* (Cambridge, Mass.: Ballinger, 1988).

18. See Manuel Castells, Lee Goh, and R.W.Y. Kwok, *The Shek Kip Mei Syndrome: Economic Development and Public Policy in Hong Kong and Singapore* (London: Pion, 1990).

19. See Tom Forester, *High Tech Society* (Oxford: Basil Blackwell, 1987).

20. See Manuel Castells et al., *Nuevas tecnologías, economía y sociedad en España* (Madrid: Alianza Editorial, 1986).

21. See François Bar, "Configuring the Telecommunications Infrastructure for the Computer Age: The Economics of Network Control" (Ph.D. diss., University of California–Berkeley, 1990).

movement similar to that which lay behind the construction of the railways and the formation of national markets during the nineteenth century. The fact that new information technologies are available at the very moment when the organization of economic activity relies increasingly on the processing of a vast amount of information, moreover, contributes to removing the fundamental obstacle to labor-productivity growth as economies evolve from material production to information processing as the source of employment for most workers. In the United States, the differential of productivity growth between information jobs and noninformation jobs increased until 1980; thereafter, however, the trend was projected to turn around as new information technologies diffused throughout the economy.[22] Furthermore, these information technologies are also the critical factor allowing for flexibility and decentralization in production and management: production and trade units can function autonomously yet be reintegrated functionally through information networks, constituting in fact a new type of economic space, which I have called "the space of flows."[23]

Thus, with the revolution in information technology as the material basis of the emerging system, the various features of structural economic transformation that we have identified relate closely to each other. In fact, they join together to form a new type of economy that I, along with a growing number of economists and sociologists,[24] propose to call the "informational economy"[25] because, at its core, the fundamental source of wealth generation lies in an ability to create new knowledge and apply it to every realm of human activity by means of enhanced technological and organizational procedures of information processing.[26] The informational economy tends to be, in its essence, a global economy; and its structure and logic define, within the emerging world order, a new international division of labor.

22. See C. Jonscher, "Information Resources and Economic Productivity," *Information Economics and Policy* 2, no. 1 (1983): 13–35.

23. See Manuel Castells, *The Informational City: Information Technology, Economic Restructuring, and the Urban-Regional Process* (Oxford: Basil Blackwell, 1989).

24. See J. Beniger, *The Control Revolution: Technological and Economic Origins of the Information Society* (Cambridge: Harvard University Press, 1986); and "Prospettive sociologiche per la società postindustriale. Lo scenario internazionale," *Sociologia* (Rome), no. 1 (1989).

25. I prefer "informational economy" to Daniel Bell's "postindustrial society" because it gives substantive content to an otherwise purely descriptive notion.

26. See Ralph Landau and Nathan Rosenberg (eds.), *The Positive Sum Strategy: Harnessing Technology for Economic Growth* (Washington, D.C.: National Academy Press, 1986).

THE NEW INTERNATIONAL DIVISION OF LABOR, THE END OF THE THIRD WORLD, AND THE RISE OF THE FOURTH WORLD

The informational economy develops on a planetary scale. But its expansion is uneven, thus originating a new international division of labor between countries and economic macroregions, one that will shape the evolution of the world economy in the coming decade. Analysis of the new international division of labor, however, has often been cast in extremely simplistic terms, leading to serious mistakes in international and national economic policies. Thus we must take a hard, analytical look at the recent dynamics of the international economy, paying special attention to those factors which account for the differential competitiveness of nations in an increasingly interdependent world market.

The experience of the past twenty-five years seems to indicate that, beyond the variations of business cycles, four principal factors are responsible for the success of nations and/or economic regions in winning market share and fostering economic growth.[27] First of all, there is the technological capacity of the productive structure of a given economy, in line with the overall transformation of the economic system toward the new logic of the information economy. Thus, econometric studies by Dosi and Soete[28] have provided evidence of the correlation between the technological level of industrial sectors and their competitiveness in international trade for all member countries of the OECD (Organization for Economic Cooperation and Development). Using the same data, they have also shown that there is no correlation between labor costs and competitiveness. Castells and Tyson[29] have reviewed comparative evidence on the differential competitiveness of Third World countries in the international economy, showing both the extremely uneven distribution of science and

---

27. See Gerard Lafay and Colette Herzog, *Commerce international. La fin des avantages acquis* (Paris: Economica, for Centre d'Etudes Prospectives et d'Informations Internationales, 1989); Stephen Cohen, David Teece, Laura D'Andrea Tyson, and John Zysman, *Competitiveness*, Vol. 3: *Global Competition: The New Reality*, the Report of the President's Commission of Industrial Competitiveness (Washington, D.C.: GPO, 1985); John Dunning (ed.), *Multinational Enterprises, Economic Structure, and Economic Competitiveness* (Chichester: John Wiley & Sons, 1988); and Robert B. Reich, *The Work of Nations* (New York: Random House, 1991).

28. Giovanni Dosi and Luc Soete, "Technology, Competitiveness, and International Trade," *Econometrica* (1983): 3.

29. Manuel Castells and Laura D'Andrea Tyson, "High Technology Choices Ahead: Restructuring Interdependence," in John Sewell and Stuart Tucker (eds.), *Growth, Exports, and Jobs in*

technology throughout the world and the importance of technological modernization in explaining differentials of competitiveness for developing countries in the open world economy.

Second, access to a large, integrated, expanding market, such as the United States, the European Economic Area (EEA),[30] or Japan, seems to be a fundamental factor in determining competitiveness.[31] This must be interpreted both as the capacity to operate in a somewhat protected domestic (or intraregional) market and as the possibility of having access to other large markets. Thus, the larger and deeper the economic integration of a given economic zone, the greater the chances of spurring productivity and profitability for the firms locating in that zone. But it is important also to underscore that the best possible combination for competitiveness for a given area is to be domestically protected from competition while having access to other large, integrated zones.[32]

Third, another important factor in explaining competitive performance in the world market is the differential between production costs at the production site and prices in the market of destination—a calculation that is more appropriate than a simplistic formula relying on labor costs, since other very important cost factors are involved (e.g., land costs, taxes, and environmental regulation).[33] However, this factor is critical only in relation to the two preceding factors. That is, the potential profit involved in the differential can be realized only if there is access to a large, rich market. Also, cost/price differentials are specific to a given technological level for the traded good: for a computer to be cheap, for example, it must first of all be a reliable computer. Since higher-value-added commodities have become increasingly important in the overall trade structure, it would seem that comparative advantages linked to differential technological capacity precede and frame the specific effect of cost/price differentials.[34]

a Changing World Economy (Washington, D.C.: Transaction Books, for Overseas Development Council, 1988).

30. The EEA combines the European Economic Community (EEC) and the European Free-Trade Association (EFTA).

31. See Laura D'Andrea Tyson, William T. Dickens, and John Zysman (eds.), The Dynamics of Trade and Employment (Cambridge, Mass.: Ballinger, 1988).

32. See Cohen et al., Global Competition.

33. See Edward K. Y. Chen, The Newly Industrializing Countries in Asia: Growth Experience and Prospects (Hong Kong: University of Hong Kong, Center for Asian Studies, 1985); and Bela Belassa et al., Toward Renewed Economic Growth in Latin America (Washington, D.C.: Institute for International Economics, 1986).

34. See Giovanni Dosi et al., Technical Change and Economic Theory (London: Pinter, 1988).

Finally, competitiveness in the new informational, global economy seems to be highly dependent on the political capacity of national and supranational institutions to steer the growth strategy of those countries or areas under their jurisdiction, including the creation of comparative advantages in the world market for those firms which are considered to represent the interests of the national and supranational collectivities underlying such political institutions. To use Chalmers Johnson's terminology, the "developmental state"[35] has played a fundamental role in affecting the transformation of the world economic structure in recent years.

These four factors, working together in close interaction, seem to account for much of the transformation of the international economy. Let us first outline the main characteristics of such transformation, leaving it for later to concentrate on the elements that may determine its future dynamics. To examine empirically the transformation of the world economy over the past twenty-five years I will use a source that, although its data are limited to the period from 1967 to 1986, organizes those data in a way permitting comparison on a homogenous basis at the level of the world's economic regions. Also, the dependability of the source assures us of a reasonably solid foundation. Our source is a study conducted by the Paris-based Centre d'Etudes Prospectives et d'Informations Internationales (CEPII) and making use of that organization's data bank, known as "CHELEM" (from the French "Comptes Harmonises sur les Echanges et l'Economie Mondiale").[36]

I have considered it more rigorous to rely on this single source, despite the obvious risks, than to refer to various data sources that are not necessarily comparable for different variables and different countries. The reader should, however, keep in mind that in the past six years (1987–92)—not included in this data base—several important transformations have taken place in the structure of the world economy: the increasing integration of the EEC and the signing of a common market agreement with EFTA to form the European Economic Area; the disintegration of the Soviet Union and the end of the Comecon; the new commercial treaties between the United States on the one hand and Canada and Mexico on the other, preparing for a future North American integration; and the growing economic interdependence between Japan and the Asian Pacific

35. See Chalmers Johnson, *MITI and the Japanese Miracle* (Stanford: Stanford University Press, 1982).
36. Lafay and Herzog, *Commerce international.*

economies. Yet, careful observation of the structural evolution of the world economy during the critical years 1967–86 seems to yield clues for understanding its transformation at the end of the present century.

(1) The first major transformation concerns the growing interdependency of the global economy, albeit within the limits of the preservation of substantial, distinctive cleavages between major economic areas which operate as trading blocs. In fact, if we distinguish major economic zones in the world, following the CEPII's calculations, intrazone trade increased from 37.6 percent of total world trade in 1967 to 40.5 percent of the world total in 1986. Thus, we have, at the same time, the marking out of macroregions in the world economy and a growing cross-regional pattern of investment, location of firms, exports, and imports, with substantial differences in the degree of penetration of each region by capital, goods, and services from other regions.

(2) At the core of the world economy, North America, Japan, and the EEC-EEA constitute the three fundamental economic regions,[37] to the extent that the rest of the world seems to be increasingly dependent upon its ability to link up with these centers of capital, technology, and market potential. One basic trend has been an evolution, in the relationship among these three macroregions, from U.S. hegemony toward multipolarity. Table 2.1 shows the decreasing contribution of the U.S. economy to world production and the increasing contribution from Japan. The EEC's share of world production also declined during that period, although the process of European market integration has lent more meaning to its presence in the world economy: an integrated 22.9 percent of the world's production in 1986 carries more weight than a simple statistical addition amounting to 26.3 percent in 1967. It cannot go without notice that the truly spectacular growth as a share of world production—greater even than that of Japan—is in "Developing Asia," which includes the Pacific Basin's newly industrialized countries (NICs) but also China (which, owing to its sheer size, is in fact statistically responsible for most of the region's growth). The "Developing Asia" region, according to the CEPII data, represented 17.4 percent of world production in 1986, compared to 7.7 percent for Japan. This is a crucial point to which we shall return.

Factors that have been proposed as crucial in this changing dynamics of competition among the core economies are measured by the export

37. See Kenichi Ohmae, *Triad Power: The Coming Shape of Global Competition* (New York: The Free Press, 1985).

Table 2.1. Share of World Economic Regions and Countries in World Output

GDP at international prices and equivalence of purchasing power in 1980	Billions of U.S.$ 1986	Structure in % 1967	1973	1980	1986
USA	3,215.2	25.8	23.1	21.3	21.4
France	517.3	3.8	3.8	3.7	3.4
Belgium-Luxembourg	94.6	0.7	0.7	0.7	0.6
Western Germany	628.4	5	4.9	4.6	4.2
Italy	525.1	3.9	3.9	3.7	3.5
Netherlands	136.8	1.1	1.1	1	0.9
U.K.	530.1	4.8	4.3	3.7	3.5
Scandinavia	247.9	1.9	1.8	1.7	1.6
Alpine Countries	139.6	1.2	1.1	1	0.9
Southern Europe	616.3	3.8	4.1	4.2	4.1
Western Europe	3,436.1	26.3	25.7	24.4	22.9
Canada	330.6	2.1	2.1	2.2	2.2
Australia and New Zealand	176.6	1.2	1.3	1.2	1.2
South Africa	96.5	0.8	0.7	0.7	0.6
CANZAS	603.7	4.1	4.1	4.1	4
Japan	1,160.6	5.8	7.2	7.4	7.7
Indonesia	192.5	0.7	0.9	1.2	1.3
India	488.3	3	2.7	2.8	3.2
Newly Industrializing Countries of Asia	322.7	0.9	1.2	1.6	2.1
Other Asian Countries	451.3	2.4	2.4	2.8	3
China	1,167.2	3.8	4.6	5.4	7.8
Indochina	non disp.	n.d.	n.d.	n.d.	n.d.
Developing Asia	2,622.0	10.8	11.8	13.8	17.4
Venezuela-Ecuador	94.8	0.7	0.7	0.7	0.6
Mexico	273.2	1.5	1.7	2.1	1.8
Brazil	426.5	1.6	2.2	2.9	2.8
Other Latin American Countries	401.6	3.1	3	3.1	2.7
Latin America	1,196.1	6.9	7.6	8.8	7.9
Persian Gulf Region	315.1	1.8	2.4	2.5	2.1
Algeria-Libya	73.4	0.4	0.4	0.5	0.5
Non-OPEC North Africa	117.7	0.6	0.6	0.8	0.8
Non-OPEC Middle East	58	0.3	0.3	0.4	0.4
Nigeria-Gabon	62.3	0.4	0.6	0.6	0.4
Other African Countries	147.2	1.2	1.1	1	1
Developing Africa	458.6	2.9	3	3.3	3.1
Soviet Union	1,475.0	11	10.8	10.3	9.8
Central Europe	553.3	4.6	4.3	4.1	3.7
All Eastern Europe	2,028.3	15.6	15.1	14.4	13.5
WORLD TOTAL	15,035.7	100	100	100	100

performance of manufacturing industries (Table 2.2) and by relative position in electronics production and in high-technology production across countries and economic zones, largely explaining the growing differential in the current balance between Japan and Western Europe, on the one hand, and the United States and most of the Third World, on the

Table 2.2. Classification of World Regions and Countries According to Their Performance in Manufacturing Exports in 1967–86

(in 1/1000 parts of world trade)	1973/67	1980/73	1986/80
Japan	15.6	9.0	10.4
Newly Industrializing Countries of Asia	14.7	17.0	9.4
Western Germany	9.0	− 17.4	6.6
Southern Europe	6.1	4.0	5.5
Italy	− 8.7	4.9	4.4
China	− 0.6	0.5	4.2
Alpine Countries	− 1.8	0.7	2.8
Brazil	5.0	3.3	2.0
Netherlands	0.7	− 4.0	1.5
Algeria-Libya	− 0.6	—	0.9
Indonesia	0.4	0.5	0.8
Scandinavia	− 1.5	− 3.1	0.5
Mexico	1.8	− 0.2	0.2
Non-OPEC Middle East	0.2	− 0.7	0.2
Non-OPEC North Africa	− 1.2	− 0.4	0.1
Persian Gulf Region	0.9	0.7	—
Nigeria-Gabon	− 0.2	− 0.1	—
Other Asian Countries	− 0.4	4.0	− 0.1
Venezuela-Ecuador	0.1	0.5	− 0.2
All Eastern Europe	4.1	0.8	− 0.4
Other African Countries	− 1.9	− 1.9	− 0.7
India	− 0.9	− 0.9	− 0.8
Other Latin American Countries	− 2.7	0.6	− 1.5
Belgium-Luxembourg	2.7	− 6.7	− 1.6
South Africa	− 1.8	1.5	− 1.9
Australia-New Zealand	3.8	− 4.2	− 2.2
Canada	− 5.4	− 4.3	− 3.4
France	2.5	− 3.0	− 4.4
U.K.	− 17.8	2.0	− 13.1
USA	− 22.9	1.5	− 21.1

*For each subperiod, variation in gains or losses in markets for commodities of the industries studied in the CHELEM data base.

SOURCE: CEPII, CHELEM data base on international trade, 1989.

other. By all possible measures, we can indeed speak of a dramatic decline in the U.S. position along with a seemingly irresistible ascent by Japan and the Asian Pacific region, with Europe improving its position relative both to itself and to the United States (but clearly lagging in the pace of growth vis-à-vis its Pacific competition, probably because of a combination of technological dependency, imperfect market integration, and indecisive political decisionmaking institutions at the supranational level). The center of the world economy, then, is gradually shifting toward the Pacific Basin, although the new impulse of European integration in 1993 could reverse the trend.

(3) The informational economy is also affecting North-South economic relations in a fundamental way and through very different processes, depending upon the country and region, to the point that today we can speak of *the end of the Third World as a relatively homogeneous economic region*.[38] At the root of this increasing differentiation lie the emergence of a new international division of labor, the shift to a new model of economic growth (characterized by the critical role of technology and the outward orientation of dependent economies as factors favoring growth), and the varying capacity of countries to engage themselves in this new growth model by linking up with world economic processes. Let us examine the evolution of the so-called Third World.

Three Development Strategies

The developing world in the post–World War II period has relied on three basic development strategies, often combined within the same country:[39] a) traditional international trade, accepting the old international division of labor, whereby raw materials and agricultural commodities were traded for manufactures and know-how in a classic pattern of unequal exchange;[40] b) import-substitution industrialization, according to the model associated with the policies articulated by CEPAL (the Spanish acronym for the UN Commission for Latin America) and designed and theorized by such leading economists as Raúl Prebisch and Aníbal Pinto;[41] and c) an outward-

38. See Nigel Harris, *The End of the Third World* (London: Penguin Books, 1986).
39. See Gary Gereffi, "Rethinking Development Theory: Insights from East Asia and Latin America," *Sociological Forum* 4 (1989): 505–35.
40. See Arghiri Emmanuel, *L'Echange inégal* (Paris: Maspero, 1973).
41. See Alain Touraine, *La Parole et le sang. Politique et société en Amerique Latine* (Paris: Odile Jacob, 1988).

figure out what will sell in international market + produce internal capital
imports @ x to figure... rather trying... report worried

oriented development strategy, taking advantage of cost/price differentials and focusing either on exports from domestic manufacturing firms (e.g., South Korea, Hong Kong, Taiwan, and Brazil) or, less often, on exports from offshore manufacturing facilities of multinational corporations (e.g., northern Mexico, Malaysia, and Singapore).[42] I argue, for the sake of simplicity, that the first development model collapsed in the 1960s, the second in the 1970s, and the third in the 1980s (with all due acknowledgment to the exceptions of individual countries and regions).[43] It does not follow that only those countries and regions which have been able and/or will be able to adapt to the new conditions of a worldwide informational economy will improve their situation and will be able to transform the current international economy. Let us briefly examine the empirical basis of our hypothesis.

Concerning the traditional international division of labor (primary commodities versus manufactured goods), the critical element is the transformation of the structure of world trade and production. As shown in Table 2.3, agriculture and mining have both lagged substantially in

Table 2.3. Volume Growth of World Merchandise Trade and Production by Major Product Group, 1960–1986 (Average Annual Percent Change)

	1960–70	1970–80	1980–86	1985	1986
Exports					
Agriculture	4.0	4.5	1.0	0	−1.0
Mining	7.0	1.5	−1.5	−2.0	7.5
Manufacturing	10.5	7.0	4.5	5.0	3.0
All merchandise	8.5	5.0	3.0	3.5	3.5
Production					
Agriculture	2.5	2.0	2.5	2.0	1.0
Mining	5.5	2.5	−1.5	1.0	6.0
Manufacturing	7.5	4.5	2.5	3.5	3.5
All merchandise	6.0	4.0	2.0	3.0	3.0

SOURCE: GATT, *Report on International Trade, 1980–1987* (Geneva: GATT, 1987).

42. See Frederic Deyo (ed.), *The Political Economy of New Asian Industrialism* (Ithaca: Cornell University Press, 1987).
43. For a general discussion of new issues in development theory and practice, see Alejandro Portes and A. Douglas Kincaid, "Sociology and Development in the 1990s: Critical Challenges and Empirical Trends"; Gary Gereffi, "Rethinking Development Theory: Insight from East Asia and Latin America"; and Peter Evans, "Predatory, Developmental, and Other Apparatuses: A Comparative Political Economy Perspective on the Third World State"—all in *Sociological Forum* 4, no. 4 (1989), a special issue.

relation to the expansion of manufacturing. Thus, with some exceptions (most notably in countries with energy resources), specialization outside manufacturing leads to a growing deterioration of the terms of trade. In addition, the general deterioration of primary commodity prices (see Table 2.4), likely to worsen by the end of the century, destroys the economic foundation for a simple survival strategy.

Import-substitution strategy and models for economic growth based on the domestic market have been the cornerstone of left-wing development theory.[44] Indeed, such thinking has played a major role in successful industrialization programs throughout Latin America (most notably in Mexico, Brazil, and Argentina)[45] and in Asia (China and India). Thus, it is not true, as neoconservative economists argue, that only an outward-looking economy can foster economic growth. Even South Korea had a very strong import-substitution policy in the 1960s, and it held onto substantial protectionist measures all along the development process.[46] However, the import-substitution model that was relatively successful in the 1950s and 1960s, particularly in Latin America, faced a crisis in the 1970s, owing to the "oil shocks," rampant inflation, and a weakening of domestic demand when the primary export sectors could not generate enough revenue to fuel the government machine and redistribute export earnings (or royalties) throughout the economy.[47]

Extravagant military expenditures and the economic disruption caused by political unrest (however justified) certainly made things worse. By 1980, in Latin America, only those countries which had emphasized an export-oriented strategy—particularly Brazil, Mexico, and Chile—were able to sustain high rates of economic growth.[48]

In fact, a new model of development had emerged in East Asia, spreading to South and Southeast Asia and then to Latin America. Now, by taking advantage of cost/price differentials vis-à-vis the developed economies, the export of manufactures would be made competitive.[49]

---

44. See Fernando Calderón, *Los movimientos sociales ante las crisis* (Buenos Aires: CLACSO, 1986).

45. See Fernando H. Cardoso and Enzo Faletto, *Dependencia y desarrollo en América Latina* (Mexico: Siglo XXI, 1969), which is available in expanded translation from the University of California Press (1979).

46. See Hyun-Chin Lim, *Dependent Development in Korea, 1963–1979* (Seoul: Seoul University Press, 1985).

47. See Fernando Fajnzylber, *La industrialización truncada de América Latina* (Mexico: Nueva Imagen, 1983).

48. See Celso Furtado, *A Nova Dependência* (Rio de Janeiro: Paz e Terra, 1983).

49. Fernando Fajnzylber, "Las economías neoindustriales en el sistema centro-periferia de los ochenta," *Pensamiento Iberoamericano* 9 (1986): 125–72.

Table 2.4. World Consumption and Prices of Major Raw Materials, 1969/71–2000

	Average Annual Rates of Growth In Consumption %				Price[b] $U.S. (Constant)			
	1969/71–1979/81	1979/81–1984/86	Projected 1984/86–2000	Unit	1969/71	1979/81	1985	Projected 2000
Agricultural nonfood[c]	1.99	.66	1.42	⋮	⋮	⋮	⋮	⋮
Cotton	1.81	1.78	1.52	lb.	1.72	1.51	1.56	1.38
Jute	1.06	−.74	1.43	m.t.	7.76	3.21	5.83	3.00
Natural rubber	2.31	2.07	2.22	lb.	.61	.64	.42	.50
Tobacco	2.15	1.96	1.68	lb.	1.21	1.01	.86	.79
Timber	2.04	−.62	1.13	lb.				
Metals and minerals[c]	2.75	.61	1.32	⋮	⋮	⋮	⋮	⋮
Copper	2.49	.86	1.44	lb.	1.66	.88	.64	.73
Iron ore	2.01	−.43	.68	m.t.	37.00	24.00	23.00	14.00
Tin	.22	−3.21	−1.05	lb.	4.33	6.75	5.41	3.34
Nickel	2.83	.97	1.06	lb.	3.38	2.75	2.23	1.69
Bauxite	4.21	.14	1.95	m.t.	33.00	39.00	30.00	26.00
Lead	1.52	.21	.42	lb.	.35	.43	.18	.17
Zinc	1.31	1.84	1.27	lb.	.37	.35	.36	.36

SOURCE: World Bank, *Price Prospects for Major Primary Commodities* (Washington, D.C.: World Bank, October 1986), vols. 1, 3, and 4, annex tables.

NOTE: Foods, beverages, and fuels are excluded.

[a]Evaluated in 1979/81 average prices.

[b]Average price. Current dollars deflated by manufacturing unit value index: 1985 = 100.

[c]Weighted average.

Certainly this was the experience of Asia's "four tigers" at the beginning of their development process, but it also extended to India (where, in the 1980s, manufactured goods exceeded 60 percent of total exports), the Philippines (81 percent), Pakistan (78 percent), Thailand (64 percent), and, after the "open door" policy was initiated in 1979, China.[50] This is the model associated with the so-called theory of the new international division of labor, which, in its most dogmatic manifestation, erroneously attributes such international division of labor to the decentralization of multinational corporations throughout the Third World.[51] (This is only one element of the model, and not the dominant one.)

It is important to realize that this model was *not* based on a sectoral specialization between developed and developing economies, but on a division of labor between high-level and low-level technological components within each product group. Thus, as Table 2.5 shows, most manufacturing trade between developed and developing countries takes place within product groups, and the importance of intra–product group trade has substantially increased over time. To understand this is critical for the purpose of our analysis because therein lies the key to understanding the crisis associated with the model.

Indeed, during the 1980s, while some regions of some countries did thrive on the basis of the model of low production costs at the low end of the manufacturing world assembly line (e.g., the Bangkok area or the *maquiladora* industries in northern Mexico), most other industrializing countries, particularly in Latin America, suffered a severe crisis and seemed to lose ground in their race to connect productively with the world economy. Two factors combined to create a major obstacle to development in a decisive moment of the development process: one a conjunctural circumstance and one a structural impediment.

Structurally, the continuous upgrading of the technological component of manufacturing products and processes required a leap forward in order to keep up with international competition. Cheap labor was not a sufficient comparative advantage when automation could easily replace unskilled labor while also improving quality.[52] Relatively low-cost labor combined

50. See Manuel Castells, "High Technology and the New International Division of Labour," *International Labour Review* (October 1989).

51. See Folker Frobel, Jürgen Heinrichs, and Otto Kreye, *The New International Division of Labor* (New York: Cambridge University Press, 1981).

52. Manuel Castells and Laura D'Andrea Tyson, "High Technology and the Changing International Division of Production: Implications for the U.S. Economy," in Randall B. Purcell (ed.), *The Newly Industrializing Countries in the World Economy: Challenges for U.S. Policy* (Boulder, Colo.: Lynne Rienner, 1989), pp. 13–50.

Table 2.5. The Growing Importance of Trade Within Product Groups in the Trade of the Developing Areas with the Developed Countries, 1970–1986

	1970	1980	1986
Textiles	66	85	94
Household appliances	35	68	92
Raw materials	52	71	91
Nonferrous metals	35	71	84
Office and telecommunication equipment	22	68	84
Other semimanufactures	55	61	84
Food	63	97	79
Other consumer goods	95	99	68
Ores and minerals	24	39	57
Iron and steel	19	21	49
Other machinery and transport equipment	12	22	45
Chemicals	17	28	35
Road vehicles	2	5	29
Clothing	47	30	17
Machinery for specialized industries	2	6	17
Fuels	8	5	13

SOURCE: GATT, *Report on International Trade, 1980–1987* (Geneva: GATT, 1987).

NOTE: For all product groups except food, clothing, and other consumer goods, the dollar values of exports and imports in the trade of the developing areas with the developed countries have become more balanced over time. This development is evident from the indexes presented. For each of the sixteen product groups shown in this table, the figures are calculated by taking the absolute amount of net trade of the developing areas with the developed countries (i.e., exports minus imports, ignoring the question of whether it is a trade surplus or a trade deficit) as a percentage of gross trade (i.e., exports plus imports), and adjusting it so that it becomes 100 if the dollar value of imports of an individual category precisely matches the dollar value of exports of that category (all figures are calculated on an f.o.b. basis). It becomes zero if there are only exports or only imports.

For example, in 1986 the developing areas exported chemicals worth $6.9 billion to the developed countries and imported chemicals worth $32.9 billion from them. The amount of net trade in chemicals was thus $26 billion, and gross trade was $39.8 billion. Net trade as a percentage of gross trade was 65 percent. The index represents the difference between that percentage and 100: namely, 35. Thus, an increase over time in the percentages in the table indicates that trade in the particular product category is becoming more balanced (i.e., net trade is becoming proportionately smaller)—a sign that countries are specializing more within the particular product category.

with automation and with a higher technological component was the winning formula. This was particularly so for those Pacific Asian NICs which made the technological transition, actually becoming competitive worldwide in the low-middle range of electronic products and rapidly winning market share in high-technology international trade.[53] Other countries, such as Argentina, did not even try, and saw their exports substantially decline (in the case of Argentina, from an average annual rate of growth of 4.7 percent in 1966–80 to − .3 percent in 1980–87).

Other countries did try conversion into higher-value-added manufacturing exports, and failed. Partly they failed because the technological leap forward was far beyond their reach—not only in terms of their ability to license new technologies, but in terms of the required overall revamping of industrial structure and productive infrastructure, including education and training, telecommunications, and communications. Partly they failed because of the conjunctural element of the foreign debt burden, which had a critical impact on the inability of many developing nations to restructure their economies at the historical moment when it was most needed. Service of the debt, together with the austerity policies imposed by lenders or international institutions, deprived many countries of substantial resources needed to modernize their economies.[54] Thus, GDP growth of the seventeen most highly indebted countries with middle- and low-income economies fell from an average annual rate of 6.1 percent in 1965–80 to 1.1 percent in 1980–87. To be sure, responsibility for the debt problem lies both in irresponsible lending by private banks during the petrodollar euphoria of the 1970s and in often wasteful use of those loans by borrowing countries. Also, within the limits of these financial constraints, many countries in the 1980s could have pursued more courageous, deliberate policies: for instance, Peru's economic catastrophe has something to do (but not everything) with the demagogy of Alan García's administration. Overall, though, it would seem that the structural effort of adaptation to the new competitive environment was so demanding that only a handful of economies and societies were able to make it by themselves. Here, the case of Brazil is much to the point.[55]

53. See Dieter Ernst and David O'Connor, *Technological Capabilities, New Technologies, and Newcomer Industrialization: An Agenda for the 1990s* (Paris: OECD Development Centre, 1990).

54. See Jacobo Schatan, *World Debt: Who Is to Pay* (London: Zed Books, 1987).

55. See Claudio R. Frischtak, "Structural Change and Trade in Brazil and in the Newly Industrializing Latin American Economies," in Purcell (ed.), *The Newly Industrializing Countries*.

In spite of all the social inequality and political inequity involved in the process, Brazil's GDP grew at an astounding average annual rate of 9 percent in 1965–80, falling to a moderate 2.7 percent annual growth in 1980–86. Particularly important in this slowdown of economic growth was the decreasing rate of export growth (from 9.4 percent to 4.3 percent annually for the corresponding periods), not to mention the drop in the investment rate: as a proportion of GDP, it fell from 22.5 percent in 1980 to 15.9 percent in 1988, thus slowing down substantially the process of industrial modernization that underlay Brazilian competitiveness. The austerity measures introduced by President Fernando Collor de Mello halted the dynamism of the Brazilian economy, which fell into negative growth in 1990 (− 4.6 percent). Thus, while Brazil remains competitive in some intermediate commodities (e.g., petrochemicals, iron and steel, aluminum), its manufacturing industry is losing competitiveness in all high-value-added sectors. Given the current movement toward privatization of the national companies and the gradual phasing out of the market reserve policy in strategic sectors, Brazil's inability to modernize the industrial structure could lead to its partial demise. The wrecking of the Brazilian economy, the only one in Latin America that had become a world-class manufacturing exporter, would signal a dramatic decline of Latin America in the world economy, underscoring the inability of a substantial part of the Third World to integrate into the new economy in the making.

On the other hand, several Latin American economies showed signs of restructuring and growth during the 1990–91 period. According to the Inter-American Development Bank, Mexico was on a path of steady growth (3.1 percent in 1989, 3.9 percent in 1990, 5.3 percent in 1991); Chile continued to grow (above 10 percent in 1989, 2.1 percent in 1990, 4.1 percent in 1991); and Argentina seemed to have recovered in 1991 (3 percent) after negative growth rates in 1989 and 1990. But Peru is literally disintegrating, with growth rates of − 11.2 percent in 1989, − 3.9 percent in 1990, and − 4.8 percent in 1991. Overall, Latin America seems to be in a state of economic uncertainty in the early 1990s. On the one hand, austerity policies have restructured the economy in some countries, albeit at a very high social cost. On the other hand, the stability of newfound growth depends largely on the ability of these more stable economies to link up with the new markets and the new production processes of the dominant economic areas. That is why Mexico, increasingly integrated into the North American economic area, and Chile, a small economy focused entirely outward, are the bright spots of the new Latin American economy. Yet, only if the region integrates internally, expanding its domestic markets, and only if the productive infrastructure undergoes a substantial process of modernization can Latin American–based firms compete and grow in the new world economy.

The foregoing analysis should afford us a better reading of the global economic evolution of the South over the past twenty-five years. In that regard, let us now examine the data provided by the World Bank in its *World Development Report, 1991.*

An Uneven Process

The story that statistics and specialized literature seem to suggest is both complex and highly varied with respect to countries, geographic regions, and time periods. Certainly it has nothing to do with the traditional left-wing imagery of a Third World that never develops. There are substantial differences in development performance between the 1965–80 period and the 1980s (the World Bank data presented here concern the period 1980–89). From 1965 to 1980, the GDP of low-income economies grew at an average annual rate of 4.8 percent, that of middle-income economies at 6.2 percent. Demographic growth substantially reduced the benefits of such economic growth, though still maintaining it at a moderately positive pace (an annual average of 2.9 percent growth for the 1965–89 period for the low-income economies). Indeed, up to 1980, the performance of Latin America as a whole was not far behind that of East Asia (7.3 percent annual growth for East Asia, 6.1 percent for Latin America); and Brazil's performance (9 percent annual growth in GDP, 9.3 percent annual growth in exports) or even Mexico's (6.5 percent and 7.6 percent, respectively) is comparable to that of the Asian role models. Albert Fishlow has provided detailed statistical evidence of comparable development paths for Latin America and East/Southeast Asia until the 1980s.[56] The big change came during the 1980s: sub-Saharan Africa and Latin America plummeted, falling from an annual GDP growth of 4.2 percent and 6.1 percent, respectively, to 2.4 percent and 1.6 percent in 1980–89 (which, in per capita terms, meant negative growth).

But even in the 1980s we must establish fundamental differences within

56. Albert Fishlow, "Economic Growth in Asia and Latin America: A Comparative Analysis" (research paper, University of California–Berkeley, 1987).

the so-called Third World. Asia, overall, maintained healthy growth during the eighties.[57] Indeed, East Asia increased its pace from 7.2 percent annual growth to 7.9 percent in the 1980–89 period; and South Asia (mainly India) improved its growth rate from 3.7 percent to 5.1 percent. Some of this Asian growth is linked to the development phenomenon known as the "saga of four tigers";[58] statistically speaking, though, the main actor of Asian development is China, which shot from a 6.9 percent average annual growth rate in real GDP (1965–80) to an astonishing 9.7 percent (1980–87). Even when we include demographic growth in our accounting, given the relative success of birth-control policies in China, per capita average annual growth for the entire 1965–89 period amounts to 5.7 percent for China, compared with 4.3 percent for Japan. (Admittedly, China's starting point was abysmally lower.) A major force in the surge of Chinese economic growth in the 1980s has been the increase in exports (10.4 percent per year in 1980–87) as the Chinese began to imitate their neighbors, following Deng Xiaoping's declaration that "it is glorious to be rich."[59] However, doubts arise about the political capacity of the Chinese regime to accomplish economic modernization without political change. Moreover, the technological and managerial upgrading of the Chinese economy, indispensable for its future competitiveness in the world market, still has a long way to go.[60]

Nevertheless, the fact that Asia as a whole has been very much on the road to development, even in the transitional 1980s, invalidates the catastrophic vision of a starving Third World, particularly when one remembers that Asia accounts for about two-thirds of the world's population. Obviously, there is widespread poverty, hunger, and sickness throughout Asia, and the process of economic growth is extremely uneven, both territorially and socially (though no more than during the European industrialization in the nineteenth century). But the basic fact remains that Asia has begun a process of economic growth that, though

57. See Carl J. Dahlman, "Structural Change and Trade in East Asia Newly Industrial Economies and Emerging Industrial Economies," in Purcell (ed.), *The Newly Industrializing Countries*, pp. 51–94.

58. See Manuel Castells, "Four Asian Tigers with a Dragon Head: A Comparative Analysis of the State, Economy, and Society in the Asian Pacific Rim," in Richard Appelbaum and Jeff Henderson (eds.), *State and Society in the Pacific Rim* (London: Sage Publications, 1992).

59. See Lynn Pan, *The New Chinese Revolution* (London: Hamish Hamilton, 1987).

60. See Patrizio Bianchi, Martin Carnoy, and Manuel Castells, *Economic Modernization and Technology Transfer in the People's Republic of China* (Stanford: CERAS, Stanford University, 1988).

fragile, could really alter the fate of this planet if that process were to be supported and consolidated at the critical moment of passage into the informational economy.

Yet, at the same time, most of Africa, the non–oil producers in the Middle East, and most of Latin America entered a structural economic crisis in the 1980s—one that could have damaging, lasting consequences for the economies and peoples of those areas, if not for all humankind. What is at issue here is not only that national economies are heavily indebted, that economic growth is sluggish or even negative, and that a substantial proportion of the population is fighting for survival every day. The critical point is that the current dramatic transformation of the world economy into a dynamic, highly integrated system could bypass entire countries or the majority of their population. The more economic growth depends on high-value-added inputs and expansion in the core markets, then the less relevant become those economies which offer limited, difficult markets and primary commodities that are either being replaced by new materials or devalued with respect to their overall contribution to the production process. With the absolute costs of labor becoming less and less important as a competitive factor (versus low labor costs relative to a certain level of technological sophistication and economic integration in the world economy), many countries and regions face a process of rapid deterioration that could lead to destructive reactions.[61] Within the framework of the new informational economy, a significant part of the world population is shifting from a structural position of exploitation to a structural position of irrelevance.

The Third World is no more—rendered meaningless by the ascendance of the newly industrialized countries (mainly in East Asia), by the development process of large continental economies on their way toward integration in the world economy (such as China and, to a lesser extent, India), and by the rise of a Fourth World, made up of marginalized economies in the retarded rural areas of three continents and in the sprawling shantytowns of African, Asian, and Latin American cities. Most of Africa has already been engulfed in this downward spiral. Latin America still struggles, with Mexico, Brazil, Argentina, Chile, Venezuela, Colombia, and Bolivia in the midst of a restructuring process that could pave the way for their articulation into the new world economy while other

61. Manuel Castells and Roberto Laserna, "The New Dependency: Technological Change and Socio-economic Restructuring in Latin America," *Sociological Forum* 4, no. 4 (1989): 535–60.

countries seem to be trapped in the fatal oscillation between hyperinflation and economic stagnation. Furthermore, a way out via self-sustaining policies seems to be excluded in a world where the sources of capital and technology are increasingly concentrated in the centers of an integrated worldwide economic system. This structural crisis, fundamentally linked to the incapacity of a number of countries (either for geographic, historical, or institutional reasons) to adapt to the new conditions of economic growth, leads to a plurality of collective reactions, all of them having high destructive potential. The first, and most straightforward, is to establish new linkages with the world economy via the criminal economy: drug production and trafficking, illegal arms deals, smuggling, and commerce in human beings (women and children in particular), or even in human organs for transplants in the private clinics of the North. We know all too well that entire societies have been entirely penetrated and restructured by criminal economic activity, prompted by high demand in the core countries and having dire consequences at both ends of the exchange.

A second reaction is the expression of utter desperation through that widespread violence, either individual or collective, which has transformed major cities in the Fourth World (and entire regions in some countries) into savage, self-destructive battlegrounds. In Africa, the collective frustration over disintegrating economies and societies often expresses itself through ancestral ethnic struggles, with the inevitable massacres and mad spirals of genocidal revenge that the rest of the world generally views with indifference.

A third reaction, rapidly developing in the Fourth World (and in some areas of the First World that could be assimilated to the special conditions of the Fourth World) is the rise of ideological/religious fundamentalism, easily associated with terrorism and/or semireligious war. The logic of exclusion embedded in the current dominant system is met with reciprocal appeals for exclusion of the dominants by the excluded. The shift from exploitation to irrelevance in some areas of the world, in relation to the dominant dynamics of the system, leads to the breakdown of any relationship and, therefore, to the alienation of entire groups, cultures, or countries from the dominant structure of the new world order. Not to be excessively mechanistic, I suggest, based on comparative observations of social dynamics over the past decade,[62] that there is a thread within the

62. Fernando Calderón and Mario R. Dos Santos (eds.), ¿Hacia un nuevo órden estatal en América Latina? (Buenos Aires: Biblioteca de Ciencias Sociales, 1988).

diversity of fundamentalist movements that have mushroomed around the world: namely, opposition to an overall model of development that threatens cultural identity as it expands across the planet while only partially reintegrating the fragments of the societies shattered by techno-economic modernization. That is to say, there is a commonality between Islamic fundamentalism, Sendero Luminoso's special brand of Maoism, and Pol Pot's Marxism-Leninism: cut all bridges with "the Other" (i.e., the developed world and its logic in the developing world), since there is little chance that the excluded can ever become true partners in a system that is so extraordinarily inclusive of economies and somewhat exclusive of societies. The instrument for cutting off such ties is the ferocious defense of territorial and cultural boundaries through unrestricted violence: Jihad against all infidels.

If the rise of the Fourth World is not counterveiled by a deliberate reform of the current world development model, the informational economy of the twenty-first century will have to reckon not only with the depressing image of starving children, but with the proliferation of powerful worldwide criminal mafias, dramatic interethnic violence, and a profound fundamentalist groundswell that will shake our tolerance and shatter our newly found peace.

THE PLACE OF THE TRANSITIONAL COMMAND ECONOMIES IN THE NEW INTERNATIONAL DIVISION OF LABOR

The end of communism as a system[63] and the rapid conversion of former command economies to market economies is a new, fundamental trend that forces us to rethink the foreseeable evolution of the international economy. The conditions of that evolution now include the gradual incorporation of the economies of Eastern Europe and the republics of the former Soviet Union.

Indeed, the Khrushchevian dream of peaceful coexistence and gradual convergence of the two systems on the basis of economic competition[64] was fulfilled, albeit in the opposite direction from his vision. Soviet

---

63. See Manuel Castells, "El fin del comunismo," *Claves* (Madrid), 1 (April 1990).
64. See *Khrushchev Remembers: The Glasnost Tapes* (Boston: Little, Brown, 1990).

production as a share of total world production declined from 11 percent in 1967 to 9.8 percent in 1986, with Eastern Europe following a parallel course from 4.6 percent to 3.7 percent.[65] The inability of the Soviet system to adapt to the conditions of the informational economy, together with the growing economic and technological differential between an integrated market economy and a stagnant pool of command economies led to piecemeal economic reforms, then to a full-fledged *perestroika*, then to the de-Sovietization of Eastern Europe and, finally, to the disintegration of the Soviet Union and the rise of a new, democratic Russia in an uncertain and unstable geopolitical era.[66]

Whatever the final outcome of such dramatic processes, the world market economy will certainly be deeply modified. The former command economies will eventually be transformed into market economies; and, in our world, this implies their full economic integration into the international system. Their sheer size and productive potential means that their incorporation will transform the current pattern of the international division of labor. Thus, our analysis would not be complete without my at least suggesting some potential future developments, notions drawn mainly from my current research on the process of technological modernization and social transformation under way in Russia.[67]

First of all, the short-term future will be dominated by a gigantic effort to revamp the productive infrastructure and to adapt existing institutions to the logic of the market economy and an open society. Such an effort is already well under way in Eastern Europe, with the possible exception of Romania, but is still in the preliminary stage in the former Soviet Union. Acute political and social instability in coming years is likely to prevent any large-scale integration effort of the former Soviet economies in the short term. Thus, for the first half of the 1990s, the most likely role to be played by the command economies in the international economy is to be

65. "CHELEM" data bank, Centre d'Etudes Prospectives et d'Informations Internationales (Paris).

66. See Padma Desai, *Perestroika in Perspective* (Princeton: Princeton University Press, 1989); Bernard Gwertzman and Michael T. Kaufman (eds.), *The Collapse of Communism* (New York: Times Books, 1990); Boris Kagarlitsky, *Farewell Perestroika: A Soviet Chronicle* (London: Verso, 1990); and Manuel Castells, *La nueva revolución rusa* (Madrid: Sistema, 1992).

67. Fieldwork in 1989, 1990, 1991, and 1992 in Moscow, St. Petersburg, and Siberia; under the auspices of the Autonomous University of Madrid, the Soviet Sociological Association, the Russian Sociological Association, the USSR Academy of Sciences, and the Russian Academy of Sciences. For preliminary results of this research project, see Manuel Castells, *La nueva revolución rusa* (Madrid: Sistema, 1992).

net recipients of Northern (i.e., Western and Japanese) capital and technology and, potentially, exporters of cheap, semiskilled labor. The border between the EEC and East European countries could well become the "Rio Grande" of Europe, as Europe's demographic decline may lead to the need for additional labor in order to sustain economic growth, and cultural barriers with the Muslim world will most likely prevent further immigration from the Southern Mediterranean region.

In a different version of the same strategy of exporting labor, strikingly reminiscent of the *maquiladora* arrangement in Mexico, European companies could set up factories on the borderline in order to lower production costs. However, preliminary assessments of the situation in Poland, as well as assessments of the conversion of East German plants, do not seem optimistic about the success of such scenarios, particularly because low-cost labor areas with much better infrastructure and more favorable institutional features still exist in the EEC, Andalusia being the most notable case in point. Still, the "Polish *maquiladoras*" option could be a reasonable scenario by the year 2000.

Second, the strongest, most likely, and most immediate connection with the world economy will be the export and joint-processing of natural resources, particularly energy resources (oil, gas, coal, and hydroelectric power—via superconductive powerlines in the not too distant future), rare metals, gold, diamonds, timber, and fish. Siberia, with its vast and only partly explored resources, is probably the critical region in this potential linkup between West and East. The rational exploitation and transport of energy resources from Siberia to Europe and Japan could provide the crucial energy source the world needs while waiting for the transition to nuclear fusion and other renewable energy sources, eliminating dependence on the always unpredictable Middle East (remember that the former Soviet Union was, in the mid-1980s, the largest producer of oil in the world). This resource-extraction development program will require a massive influx of capital, technology, machinery, and expertise and could well be the first stage of the eventual integration of the former command economies into the world economy.

A third possibility, for some East European economies around the year 2000, would be the mobilization of the scientific and technical human potential that now exists, vastly underutilized, in many areas (in Hungary and the Baltic republics, for instance). Joint ventures between Western and local firms to tap into the highly skilled labor market existing in such societies could represent a new frontier of decentralized production for

Western companies. The recent development of an active software industry in Hungary, catering to Western firms, and the spontaneous growth of a high-technology complex around the old, distinguished Tartu University in Estonia are examples of how market economies can make use of scientific potential that was being wasted under the command system.

In the midterm, between ten and twenty years from now, the critical role that such economies (particularly the economies of the various former Soviet republics) can play in the world system is to provide the expanded markets needed to match the fast-growing productive capacities of the information economy. This, however, requires that Western firms gradually infuse capital and technology into the productive fabric of Eastern Europe and the former Soviet republics, so that these economies themselves become sources of dynamism. The full incorporation of a market of 400 million consumers in the Western economy—with particular emphasis on the West European economy—will ensure the necessary outlet for an increasingly productive system as we move full speed into the informational economy over the coming two decades.

One contribution that the collapse of the Soviet system has already made to the world economy is the "peace dividend" that we can perhaps now afford. It would, of course, be utopian to pretend that we have reached the point where we can proceed with general disarmament, as the Gulf War dramatically showed. The historic transition that we are experiencing in so many dimensions of our social and economic systems is full of opportunities, but also full of dangers. Thus, democracies must be ready to resort to military force, whenever and wherever necessary: the notion of a unified, civilized world depends for its fulfillment on the determination of the civilized world to defend itself, on behalf of the whole of humankind. Therefore, leaner, smaller, more effective, high-tech-equipped, *and information-oriented* military forces must be at the disposal of all major nations, perhaps increasingly coordinated through international peacekeeping institutions. Yet, the dismantlement of the enormous military apparatus that sustained the balance of nuclear terror during the Cold War represents a fantastic saving not just of capital and equipment, but also of human, technological, and scientific resources that can now be put to use in a full-scale, globally oriented development program.

The challenges represented by the disintegration of the Second World, the end of the Third World, and the rise of the Fourth World must be taken up in the current process of restructuring our world. The opportunities and the dangers arising in such a process constitute the raw material from which are made the new social conflicts and political strategies that together will shape the world of the twenty-first century.

3

Martin Carnoy

Multinationals in a Changing World Economy: Whither the Nation-State?

Large multinational enterprises (known as MNEs)[1] continue to grow rapidly and to influence changes in the world economy. They also dominate trade among the industrialized countries[2] and control interna-

Invaluable assistance in preparing this chapter was provided by Tahir Salie and Pia Wong, graduate students at Stanford University. The author also thanks Manuel Castells, Laura D'Andrea Tyson, and Rebecca Morales for intellectual guidance and Gary Gereffi for comments on an earlier version of this chapter.

1. There are many definitions of multinational enterprises. For our purposes, I will use the definition which emphasizes that an MNE invests directly abroad and gets more than 10 percent of its revenues from foreign investments.

2. For example, in 1988, U.S. multinational companies accounted for 67 percent of total U.S. merchandise exports and 41 percent of total U.S. merchandise imports. Intracompany trade between parent companies and their offshore affiliates accounted for about 30 percent of U.S. merchandise exports and almost 20 percent of total U.S. merchandise imports. The affiliates of foreign firms in the United States accounted for 23 percent of U.S. exports and 33 percent of imports. See Laura D'Andrea Tyson, "Does a National Trade Policy Make Sense in a World of Global Corporations?" Berkeley Roundtable on the International Economy, September 13, 1990 (mimeo), p. 1. See also her *Who's Bashing Whom: Trade Conflicts in High Technology Industries* (Washington: Institute for International Economics, 1992).

tional capital movements. In the rapid informatization and internationalization of production and distribution, much of the innovation (R&D) in information technology takes place in the MNEs or is financed by them, especially as the cost of innovation has risen.[3]

According to the United Nations Centre on Transnational Corporations, which issues major periodic studies on MNEs,[4]

> Transnational corporations (TNCs) are perhaps the most important actors in the world economy. They straddle national boundaries and the biggest TNCs have sales which exceed the aggregate output of most countries. The foreign content of output, assets and employment in many of them is large, in some instances ranging from 50 percent to over 90 percent. . . . The largest 600 industrial companies account for between one-fifth and one-fourth of value added in the production of goods in the world's market economies.[5]

Their very size, financial resources, investment in research and development, and organizational capability, then, make MNEs attractive and usually necessary additions to any country's economy. This despite many potential drawbacks: on the one hand, their alleged "footloose" quality— no allegiance to national development goals—and, on the other, a high level of relative economic power (in all but the largest economies) which allows them to shape national development goals to their own needs. The "foreignness" of foreign-based multinational firms, with their headquarters (and perhaps most-profitable activities) located abroad, is also a sensitive political issue in most countries. Such drawbacks confront mainly those nation-states[6] where there is large "inward" investment by multi-

3. A great deal of innovation also takes place in small firms, as epitomized by the Silicon Valley model. But innovations by large firms, such as Du Pont, IBM, Toyota, ATT, and the Japanese electronic manufacturers, to name just a few, have been underestimated. See, for example, Michael Piore and Charles Sable, *The Great Industrial Divide* (New York: Basic Books, 1986).

4. The United Nations uses the term "transnational" rather than "multinational." But these terms should not be considered interchangeable: TNC implies that the corporation is above nationality; MNE (or MNC) implies that the corporation has businesses in more than one country but may be very "national" in certain aspects of its behavior and interests. These differences will be discussed in detail below.

5. United Nations Centre on Transnational Corporations, *Transnational Corporations and World Development*, ST/CTC/89 (New York: United Nations, 1988), p. 16.

6. "Nation-states" are defined as national political systems that can count on significant identification of the citizenry with the system.

nationals (foreign multinationals coming into a national market), but it also affects those with "outward" investment (domestic multinational firms investing in other countries), especially where the MNEs sacrifice local employment for lower labor costs abroad. Robert Reich, for one, argues that the notion of MNE "foreignness" is anachronistic in the new world economy, since there is no inherent difference between being employed by a national or foreign-based MNE except that the foreign company is likely to pay its employees more, even in the United States. His notion of the nation-state revolves around the capacity of those who live and work in the nation to produce (whether they be labor or capital owners) rather than around political identification.[7] This issue will be discussed in more detail below.

Since today's international political economy is dominated not only by MNEs but by the increasing importance of R&D-intensive industries (where MNEs are especially strong), what stance, if any, should national politics take toward them? Is there a way to work with multinationals to maximize long-term national welfare from the standpoint of lower- and middle-income citizens? Or are the aims of such large corporations inherently opposed to such "popular" or "progressive" goals? Put another way, are there very low or easily reducible potential costs to the national interest of large multinationals' domestic operations? Or are such costs very high and largely irreducible?

At the heart of the problem is the possible conflict between the ends and means of the nation-state and the ends and means of private multi-national enterprises.[8] In this context, the nature of the debate about the pros and cons of foreign investment has changed remarkably over the past twenty years. For one thing, the multinationals' increasing economic power in a world made smaller by advances in telecommunications, transportation, and international finance has enhanced their position. Their position has also been enhanced by the collapse of the most historically important countermultinational alternative—international state communism. And although multinationals continue to have legiti-

7. See Robert Reich, *The Work of Nations* (New York: Vintage, 1992). Also, Robert Reich, "Who Is Us?" *Harvard Business Review* 90, no. 1 (March–April 1990): 53–94. For a contrary view, see Tyson, "Does a National Trade Policy Make Sense?"

8. The existence of potential conflict means that the market mechanism is not an acceptable form of conflict resolution. If it were acceptable, the nation-state would allow international market prices to allocate resources worldwide, even if that were detrimental to its own citizens. Neither would the state attempt to subsidize various economic (or economy-enhancing) activities on national soil.

macy problems,[9] the legitimacy of the nation-state may have suffered even more over the past two decades, in part because of its increased difficulties with respect to producing rapid and socially equitable economic growth. This alone pushes nation-states to fall deeper into the waiting arms of technology-bearing, capital-laden, multinational firms.[10]

All this suggests that important changes in the international political economy have altered the *perception* of potential conflict between what multinationals represent and what the nation-state represents. This has changed the policy choices for nation-states. The realistic dilemma now is not *whether* to work with multinationals—it is increasingly difficult, even if it were ever desirable, for nations to keep out direct foreign investment or to prevent national companies from investing abroad—but, rather, *which policies regarding relations with multinationals will best promote a legitimate political agenda for the nation-state.* To develop such policies, national decisionmakers must have a clear idea of what multinationals are like, including 1) why they are multinationals, 2) what difference, if any, it makes to have foreign ownership of local production or to have ownership by one country's multinational versus another's, and 3) what difference, if any, it makes to have national ownership of foreign production.

THE CHANGING AND UNCHANGING ECONOMIC POWER OF MULTINATIONALS

Multinational corporations are large, and they are growing larger more rapidly than the world economy as a whole. The largest are concentrated in four economic sectors: three of these are industrial sectors—oil, autos, and electronics/high tech; the fourth is banking. Notably, one of these sectors, oil, has grown far more slowly in recent years than the others,

9. The clearest example is that of Exxon and other oil companies, with their frequent and often devastating environmental mishaps. Oil companies also engender consumer ire whenever there is an increase in gasoline prices. In the United States, "big oil" is almost universally seen as the symbol of multinational monopoly capitalism in its worst form.

10. There is some question about the willingness of MNEs to invest in many developing countries. In the 1980s, such foreign direct investment (FDI) has decreased in developing countries except from Japan. See United Nations Centre on Transnational Corporations, *Transnational Corporations.*

and oil companies have therefore not done as well, at least until the Middle East crisis of 1990–91.

It is widely accepted wisdom that multinationals are "beyond" the influence of nation-states and their economies. This turns out to be only partially true. Even though the international market variations that contribute to slower or more rapid growth of different sectors have an important effect on who wins and who loses in the international economy, some *countries'* multinationals are growing much more rapidly *irrespective* of sector.[11] The most obvious example is Japan, yet there are smaller versions of the Japanese case in Korea, Hong Kong, Singapore, and Taiwan.

Let us see how multinationals today compare as an economic force with the multinationals of the mid-1970s.

(1) Multinationals continue to grow more rapidly than the world economy.[12] In 1975, the fifty largest industrial corporations in the world (essentially all were multinationals) had $540 billion in sales and $25 billion in profits. By 1990, sales of the top fifty had reached $2.1 trillion and their profits amounted to $70 billion, down from $82 billion in 1989 (see Figure 3.1). In real terms (1975 U.S. dollars), this translates into a 3.5 percent annual sales growth between 1975 and 1990, a 3 percent growth in profits between 1975 and 1989, but, because of the poor profits in 1990, only a 1.3 percent growth in profits between 1975 and 1990. For comparison's sake, the U.S. economy grew at a 2.8 percent rate over the same period, and the economies of the OECD (Organization for Economic Cooperation and Development) averaged a 2.9 percent rate of growth. Put a different way, sales of the fifty largest industrial multinationals were 28 percent of U.S. GNP in 1975 and 39 percent of U.S. GNP in 1989.

This growth pattern was repeated even more dramatically in the banking sector. First and foremost, banking has grown very rapidly in the second half of the 1980s—more rapidly than any other major sector of economic activity. Figure 3.2 shows how assets of the largest fifty commercial banks increased in real terms by a total only of 7 percent between

11. See Michael Porter, *The Competitive Advantage of Nations* (New York: The Free Press, 1990). Porter argues that the national and regional environment in which private business operates has a profound influence on its ability to compete and to expand. In addition, the home market for MNEs is an important base of expansion.

12. In 1974, Richard Barnet and Ronald Müller wrote in *Global Reach* (New York: Simon & Schuster, 1974) that "the average growth rate of the most successful global corporations is two to three times that of the most advanced industrial countries" (p. 15). If we take the top fifty industrial multinationals, their comparative growth rate was much smaller over the past fifteen years or so.

Figure 3.1.   Total sales of the fifty largest industrial corporations in the world, by product group, 1975–1990.

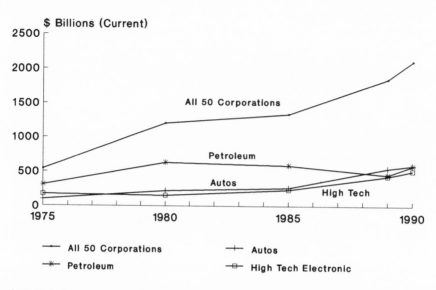

SOURCE: *Fortune.*

1980 and 1985, but increased by an astounding total 87 percent in constant dollars between 1985 and 1989.

(2) Multinationals as a whole expand and contract with the expansion and contraction of the world economy. For example, the 1980s were not particularly good years for these large companies when compared with the end of the previous decade (Figure 3.1 and 3.3),[13] mainly because of the recession in the early 1980s. Thus, even with their capacity to take advantage of opportunities outside national boundaries, as a group the industrial multinationals do only somewhat better than the major nation-state players in the international economy.

(3) That said, certain sectors (electronic/high tech, autos, and banking), and particularly some Japanese firms in those sectors, grew much more rapidly than the world economy and/or their home economies. Although U.S. firms have dominated the largest industrial sectors throughout this

13. Data for the largest one hundred corporations in the world are not available for 1975, but the similar growth pattern for the top fifty and the top hundred in the 1980s suggests that the growth rate was larger for both groups in the 1970s than in the 1980s.

Figure 3.2. Total assets of the world's fifty largest banks, by country, 1980–1990.

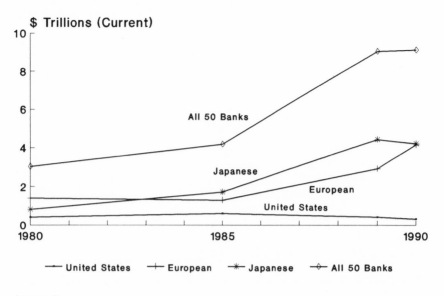

SOURCE: *Fortune.*

period, there were major differences in growth among multinationals according to country of origin. Japanese corporations have made much more rapid gains than either the U.S. or the European firms. U.S. firms have done especially poorly. *The rapid growth and increased internationalization of large Japanese firms in autos and electronics/computers—both crucial industries in the new, high-tech world economy—is the single biggest change in this fifteen-year period.* This growth has so disturbed the "old order" of a U.S.-European "equilibrium" in the world economy that some analysts even explain the drive toward a single, regional European economy as a response to this Japanese "threat."[14]

In the late 1970s and early 1980s, almost half of the largest fifty industrial corporations (twenty-three firms in 1980, twenty-one in 1985) and half the largest hundred (forty-four in 1980, forty-five in 1985) were

14. Wayne Sanholtz and John Zysman, "1992: Recasting the European Bargain," *World Politics* 42 (October 1989): 95–128. In their words, "the trigger has been a real shift in the distribution of economic power resources . . . crudely put, relative American decline and Japanese ascent" (p. 95).

Figure 3.3.   Total sales of the fifty largest industrial corporations in the world, by country, 1975–1990.

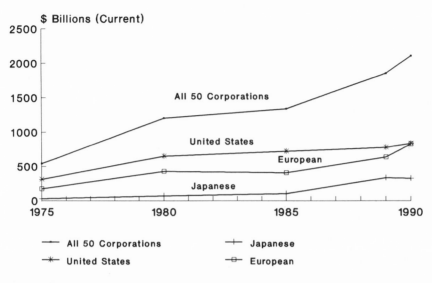

SOURCE: *Fortune.*

U.S.-based. By 1990, this number had dropped significantly. Only sixteen of the largest fifty and thirty-three of the largest hundred were American. But the number of Japanese-based industrial firms increased dramatically, from five of the top fifty in 1980 to nine in 1990, and from eight to sixteen of the top hundred. Most of this gain came in the final five years. Yet, the number of European Community and German corporations stayed about the same during this period at eighteen to twenty-one of the largest fifty (six to seven German) and thirty-eight to forty-two of the largest hundred (eleven to thirteen German).[15]

The 1980s were also marked by Japanese banking expansion. The assets of Japanese banks grew from 25 percent of the total assets of the largest fifty banks in 1980 to 57 percent of total assets in 1989, but dropped to 46 percent in 1990. European Community banks stayed constant at 46–47 percent. But the big losers were U.S. banks, whose assets grew much more slowly than their Japanese and European competitors. In part, this

15. The big surprise is that the number of German firms at the top fell in number, from seven to six of the largest fifty and from thirteen to eleven of the largest hundred.

was because of changing currency rates (particularly vis-à-vis European banks). Even in the early 1980s, though, when the dollar was strong relative to other currencies, the assets of Japan's commercial banks were growing more rapidly than those of American banks. In 1980, two of the ten largest banks in the world were American, and eight were European. By 1990, six of the largest banks were Japanese, and four were European.

(4) Despite all the talk about the "globalization" of world business, most multinationals' performance is still closely tied to the competitiveness of its "home" economy. In 1988, for example, U.S. parent operations accounted for 78 percent of the total assets, 70 percent of the total sales, and 74 percent of the total employment of U.S. multinationals. These shares were actually slightly higher than in 1977.[16] One estimate places the proportion of assets of Japanese MNEs' parent operations at 90 percent.[17] Foreign-affiliate operations may often be more profitable than the operations of the parent company—for example, Ford Motor Company's European operations were more profitable than those of the U.S. parent in the late 1980s—but their production is usually much smaller.

The obverse is also true. In the industrialized countries, foreign affiliates of multinationals also occupy a minority position overall in each domestic economy, although in many industrial economies they may dominate a particular sector. In the late 1980s, for example, foreign affiliates accounted for only 4.3 percent of all U.S. business gross product, up from 2.3 percent in 1977, and 10.5 percent of manufacturing gross product, up from 5 percent in 1977.[18] Similarly, in Japan, the share of sales and assets of foreign-affiliated enterprises in all industry was about 4.5 percent in 1980,[19] and in France foreign investment represented about 5.5 percent of gross fixed capital formation in the late 1970s.[20]

Even in Japan, however, the petroleum sector as of 1980 was dominated by foreign-affiliated firms (38 percent of sales and 62 percent of profits in

16. Tyson, "Does a National Trade Policy Make Sense?" pp. 9–10.

17. Stephen S. Cohen, "Testimony at the Joint Economic Committee of the U.S. Congress: 'Who is US—Does Corporate Nationality Matter?' " Berkeley Roundtable on the International Economy, September 5, 1990 (mimeo). The United Nations Centre on Transnational Corporations estimates that 80 percent of Japanese MNEs' employment is in Japan, but the authors of that estimate think it may well be low (*Transnational Corporations*, p. 212).

18. Cohen, "Who is US," pp. 14–15.

19. Terutomo Ozawa, "Japan," in John Dunning (ed.), *Multinational Enterprises, Economic Structure, and International Competitiveness* (New York: John Wiley, 1985), table 5.2.

20. Charles-Albert Michalet and Therese Chevalier, "France," in Dunning (ed.), *Multinational Enterprises*, p. 94.

1980). And, in a country such as France—integrated into a regional common market—about 22 percent of all manufacturing industry has more than one-fifth of its capital held by a foreign firm. In a number of France's most technology-intensive manufacturing sectors (especially in computers, agricultural machinery, chemicals, and petroleum/natural gas) foreign affiliates dominate.[21]

The fate of the domestic economy is therefore generally tied to the fate of domestically based business; and, in most cases, the fate of multinationals is at least somewhat connected to the competitiveness of their home economies. Yet many, if not most, economies—even the highly industrialized ones—rely on foreign multinationals to produce a significant array of goods for the domestic market. These goods are usually the most technology-intensive, precisely because it is advanced technology that gives the foreign MNE a worldwide specific advantage. At the same time, it is in the most technology-intensive sectors that MNEs are the most global. Table 3.1 shows that, for the United States, these high-tech sectors generally have a much higher than average proportion of assets abroad than manufacturing as a whole. A glance at Table 3.2 will show that Europe is the main theater of operations for such U.S. MNEs.

Table 3.1.   U.S. Parent Total Assets, Foreign-Affiliate Assets, and Ratio of Parent's Foreign Assets to Total Assets, 1986

Industry	U.S. Parent	Foreign Affiliate	Ratio
	$Millions		%
All manufacturing industries	1,408,850	474,697	33.7
High-tech manufacturing industries	482,815	192,575	41.6
Radio, TV & communication equipment	134,929	23,188	17.2
Electronic computers & accessories	23,450	8,130	34.7
Office & computing machines	99,249	57,838	58.3
Drugs & medicines	57,474	28,948	50.4
Industrial chemicals & synthetics	90,228	48,644	53.9
Instruments & related products	50,238	22,973	45.7
Engines & turbines	7,249	2,854	39.4
Other manufacturing industries	946,035	282,122	29.3

SOURCE: National Science Board, *Science and Engineering Indicators*, 1989 (Washington, D.C.: U.S. GPO, 1989).

21. Ibid., pp. 103–4.

Table 3.2. Country Locations of U.S. Parent Companies' Foreign Affiliates, by Industry, 1986

Industry	Total	Canada	Europe	Japan	Other Asian & Pacific	Latin America
	← $ Millions →					
All manufacturing industries	474,697	56,943	208,124	50,549	20,237	79,288
High-tech manufacturing industries	189,721	16,465	89,847	22,884	10,084	26,039
Radio, TV & communication equipment	23,188	2,019	9,835	2,324	2,974	4,272
Electronic computers & accessories	8,130	575	3,080	1,102	1,354	712
Office & computing machines	57,838	3,419	29,931	8,601	2,872	3,916
Drugs & medicines	28,948	1,871	13,775	3,421	1,016	5,968
Industrial chemicals & synthetics	48,644	7,159	20,362	3,883	1,345	8,638
Instruments & related products	22,973	1,622	12,884	3,353	503	2,533
Other manufacturing industries	284,976	40,478	118,277	27,865	10,173	53,229
	← % →					
All manufacturing industries	100.0	12.0	43.8	10.6	4.3	16.7
High-tech manufacturing industries	100.0	8.7	47.4	12.0	5.3	13.7
Radio, TV & communication equipment	100.0	8.7	42.4	10.0	12.8	16.4
Electronic computers & accessories	100.0	7.1	37.9	13.6	16.7	8.8
Office & computing machines	100.0	5.9	51.7	14.9	5.0	8.8
Drugs & medicines	100.0	5.8	47.6	11.8	3.5	20.8
Industrial chemicals & synthetics	100.0	14.7	41.9	8.0	2.8	17.8
Instruments & related products	100.0	7.1	56.0	14.6	2.2	11.0
Other manufacturng industries	100.0	14.2	41.5	9.8	3.6	18.7

SOURCE: National Science Board, *Science and Engineering Indicators*, 1989 (Washington, D.C.: U.S. GPO, 1989).

(5) The changes of the past fifteen years in MNEs were also dramatic within sectors. Two out of every three dollars of profit going to the largest one hundred industrial multinationals in 1980 were earned by oil companies. But because the decade of the 1980s was a slow growth period for natural resource firms, that percentage had dropped to less than 25 percent by 1989. In 1980, thirty of the top hundred industrial firms were oil companies—with $41 billion in profits. In 1989, there were only seventeen in the top hundred, with only $25 billion in profits ($17 billion in 1980 dollars).[22] The opposite trend occurred in other sectors. During the 1980s, the number of automobile producers in the top hundred industrials rose from ten to fifteen (from nine to eleven in the top fifty). But, more important, their sales increased at almost 6 percent annually, and negative profits in 1980 (mainly owing to huge losses by the U.S. auto companies) became $23 billion in profits in 1989, almost equal to those from oil. General Motors and Ford have remained the largest of the auto producers (and were the largest corporations in the world in 1989), yet the fastest growing companies are Japanese, especially Toyota, Nissan, Honda, and Mazda. In 1980, Toyota's sales were 24 percent of GM's; in 1989, they had leaped to 47 percent. Nissan's growth was much slower (from 23 percent to 28 percent of GM's sales), but Honda jumped from 12 to 21 percent. Certain other auto companies, such as Daimler-Benz, also showed enormous growth during the late 1980s, especially in profits: after earning a steady $600 million in the early 1980s, Daimler-Benz shot to $3.5 billion in profits in 1989, ahead of all but GM and Ford.[23]

As might be expected, multinationals in consumer electronics and high tech (computers, telecommunications) also did well in the 1980s. The number of such companies in the top hundred went from fourteen to twenty-two in the 1980–90 period. Their sales (in 1980 dollars) grew at a 6.4 percent annual rate, and profits increased from $11 billion to $20 billion (in current dollars). Again, Japanese companies have done extraordinarily well: their sales in the 1980s rose at 17 percent annually in 1980 dollars, and profits grew from $1.2 billion to $6 billion (in current dollars).

22. As might be expected, most of the shrinkage was in the "smaller" U.S. oil companies. In 1980, twenty of the largest thirty companies were American; in 1989, only nine out of seventeen were.

23. Another piece of evidence that an MNE's success is rooted in the economic strength of its national economy is the disastrous performance in 1991 of the two giants, GM and Ford. Because of a sharp decline in the U.S. auto market, the two suffered their worst losses of the post–World War II period.

We have already noted the rapid growth of the banking sector since 1980, especially since 1985. The late 1980s were certainly characterized by an explosion of finance capital, and it was Japanese capital that led the way.

By 1990, then, electronics/high tech, autos, and oil together accounted for about 65 percent of the total profits of the top hundred industrials, down from about 75 percent in 1980, which had been the end of a decade dominated by the expansion of big oil (and banking). Japanese multinationals in autos and electronics expanded the most rapidly during the 1980s, and oil companies—especially U.S. oil companies—lost the most ground. European industrial companies did not do nearly as well as the Japanese, but they lost less ground to the Japanese than did the Americans. The American loss was even larger in the banking sector.

All this could change in the 1990s if petroleum prices rise radically— not a likely scenario after the Gulf War, but still possible should Russian supplies not meet growing East European demand and should economic growth pick up in the West (particularly in the United States). Oil companies would surely increase sales and profits sharply, as they did in the autumn of 1990, and this might increase the growth of U.S.-based multinationals because of their strong position in oil. American banks might also profit from an oil crisis. Auto sales (including Japanese sales) and especially profits would probably fall.

(6) There has been a dramatic increase in international cooperation agreements *among* multinationals over the past ten years.[24] This point will be discussed more in detail below, but it is worth noting here the pervasiveness across industrial sectors of strategic alliances, so much so that even small firms within countries are beginning to pursue such agreements. To some extent, strategic alliances counter the "nationalness" of multinationals: firms that ally with firms from other countries are less likely to look like companies from a particular country. But the "internationalness" of a strategic alliance is open to question. Most such alliances are focused on marketing products or acquiring specific inputs. They do not change the nature of the particular firms involved unless there is an asymmetry of power, and then it is the economically weaker firm which is changed. When Schlumberger buys Fairchild Semiconductors for its

24. See United Nations Centre on Transnational Corporations, *Transnational Corporations*, pp. 59–65. The UNCTNC emphasizes mergers and acquisition activity among MNEs and, in the electronics sector, interfirm agreements, or what others have called "strategic alliances." As I will show, interfirm cooperation on technology goes beyond electronics and telecommunications to autos and other traditional manufacturing industries.

R&D capability, it is the French buyer that dominates the relationship, even though Fairchild remains rather intact. It may make Fairchild somewhat less American, but does it make Schlumberger less French? Companies such as Siemens, IBM, and Honda would like "to quietly blend" their giant corporations into the local landscape,[25] but whether this means losing their national identity is a complex question.

WHAT ARE THE ADVANTAGES AND DISADVANTAGES OF MULTINATIONALS?

If multinationals earn higher profits than strictly national companies, it is because they are able to capture gains by operating abroad that they could not capture were they simply to export to other countries or to license to other countries' producers. This ability to capture profits worldwide is an outgrowth of the very reasons that firms become successful multinationals, and it is also the most persuasive argument both for attracting foreign multinationals to invest domestically and for domestic firms to become multinationals. These reasons fall into three categories—those which are specific to the firm, those which are specific to the industry, and those which are specific to individual country conditions.

(1) Multinationals have firm-specific assets (monopolistic advantages), such as better technologies and better managerial practices, that allow them to compete successfully with local firms in other countries.[26] At the same time, there are imperfect external markets for these firm-specific assets, so that the firm cannot sell them to local producers for a price that matches what they can get by controlling the asset directly. The biggest problem arises from a dynamic, technologically changing world, where it is impossible to draft a complete contract that covers the risks and uncertainty associated with rapid change. Such contractual uncertainties

25. Mark Goldstein, "Siemens: Foreign Giant with a Low Profile," *Industry Week*, January 16, 1989, p. 22.

26. See Richard Caves, "International Corporations: The Industrial Economics of Foreign Investment," *Economica* 38, no. 149 (1971): 1–27. Summarizing a series of industry case studies, Gary Gereffi and Richard Newfarmer conclude that "the positions of dominance of TNCs in international markets are rooted in monopolistic advantages protected by barriers to entry at home and abroad." See Gereffi and Newfarmer, "International Oligopoly and Uneven Development: Some Lessons from Industrial Case Studies," in Richard Newfarmer (ed.), *Profits, Progress, and Poverty* (South Bend: Notre Dame University Press, 1985), p. 386.

raise the "transaction cost" of licensing arrangements relative to the lower transaction cost that can be achieved within the firm, specifically by improving firm organization in a way that makes it more profitable to operate branches abroad.

Once a company has learned to operate a number of geographically dispersed operations, the internal transaction costs associated with opening new operations in other geographic locations may be very low. The firm's organization is already geared to multiregion, multinational production. Even if the transaction cost of licensing or direct export falls, therefore, those firms which have already "learned by doing" may have such low internal transaction costs that they still prefer direct ownership.

The earlier growth of multinational firms in the world economy also promoted the development of technologies that further lowered the internal transaction costs of widely dispersed operations. Improved telecommunications were combined with computers to facilitate handling much greater amounts of information much more rapidly; organizational structures particularly suited to multiple-site operations were developed; and worldwide media networks made possible the gradual universalization of consumer tastes.[27]

(2) The conditions that make for the existence of firm-specific assets whose external markets are characterized by imperfections—better technologies and managerial practices—are often associated with industries marked by a high degree of concentration, or at least by the existence of a few large, leading firms (oligopolistic competition). This correlation is caused by economies of scale in R&D costs, and, although it was thought that small firms have an advantage in organizational innovation,[28] the probably even greater advantage of large firms to organize themselves for reducing financial and marketing costs.

Conversely, one reason to operate as a multinational rather than to export or license is that there are economies of scale associated with that industry, and direct ownership of production abroad allows for the realization of those economies.[29] In some industries, there are possibilities of creating bilateral monopolies by investing directly (a monopoly in each of several countries). The high degree of concentration may also create

27. If business culture became universal at the same rate as consumer tastes, there would be no advantage for the multinational firm, since international contracting would become cheaper as rapidly as the marketing knowledge specific to the multinational firm became more valuable.
28. See Piore and Sable, *The Great Industrial Divide*.
29. See Dunning (ed.), *Multinational Enterprises*.

conditions that promote vertical integration, and direct ownership provides the greatest control over the supply of crucial inputs. Both Ford and General Motors have established large, highly productive plants in Mexico and Canada that supply engines for several different vehicle models in final assembly, also at different locations.[30] GM's foray into the Saturn car, manufactured and assembled at various global locations, is the logical outcome of a vertical integration that takes advantage of low-cost production locations but maintains control over supply (and quality of supply) within the company.

(3) Another set of factors that favor multinationalization are specific to individual countries. As countries attempt to restrict trade, for example, or to increase regulations on particular products, the general effect will be to increase the costs of using external markets relative to multinational control.[31] Most countries have, in fact, implemented policies that promote foreign investment by restricting trade.[32] A good example is the historically rather high protection of local production by European countries. Early on, U.S. auto producers invested in Europe, whereas European producers (and, later, the Japanese) exported to the United States. More recently, U.S. computer firms have moved final production into European markets. U.S. quotas on Japanese automobiles have prompted Honda and Toyota to move their small-car, U.S.-destined production to the United States. National regulations on drugs and banking have likewise prompted direct foreign investment in those industries in order to conform at lower cost to local conditions.

Some countries have implemented specific legal and fiscal policies or forms of direct subsidy in order to attract foreign investment. In today's Poland, local firms in a variety of industries are guaranteed a three-year tax holiday if they form a joint-venture with foreign capital. Some years earlier, Malaysia gave massive tax and utility concessions to foreign firms to establish chip, automobile, and other production plants there.

30. See Harley Shaiken, *Mexico in the Global Economy: High Technology and Work Organization in Export Industry* (La Jolla: University of California–San Diego, Center for U.S.-Mexican Studies, 1990).

31. Jeremy Clegg, *Multinational Enterprise and World Competition* (London: Macmillan, 1987), p. 20.

32. Direct foreign investment can also be restricted, however, as the Japanese have shown. Their policy has been to promote licensing rather than foreign investment. Brazil's "market reserve" policy restricted foreign investment in the minicomputer and personal computer industry as well as trade. Both these countries' policies effectively kept multinationals out of their markets in whatever products they wanted to protect exclusively for local firms.

Other countries have implemented policies that protect their own multinationals from foreign competition at home or that subsidize their R&D and/or foreign investments directly and indirectly. This is usually part of a neomercantile policy that aims at reducing the capability of other countries' firms to increase their own specific assets over time, especially when development of those specific assets is connected with large R&D efforts related to a potentially large market. By cutting off that market through state-supported predatory practices, one country can prevent another country's firms from expanding and becoming multinationals themselves. The international rivalry of MNEs based in different countries has seemed to erode neither the industry-specific entry barriers used to protect home-country industries nor the global concentration of those industries.[33]

Advantages to the Host Economy

When foreign multinationals invest in a local economy, they theoretically can displace domestic firms only if they possess firm-specific assets that can make the economy more productive and competitive in the long run. The main advantage for the local economy is to get the better technology and management as such firms employ workers locally, increase local production, create the demand for local inputs, and lower the price of goods to local consumers.

The advantage of multinational firms to those countries not having their own technological and management capability, therefore, is not only the fact of local production and its direct impact on economic growth, but the potential transfer of at least some of the multinationals' special assets to local producers. Even if the multinational maintains tight control over specific technologies, managerial capability and worker skills would theoretically have to be transferred through in-house training and backward linkages (local sourcing). The more willing the multinational firm is to hire local managers and to source locally, the greater the advantage to the local economy of foreign direct investment.

Those economies which have potentially large markets, a pool of trainable, low-cost, higher-skilled labor and management, good communications infrastructure (reducing intramultinational transaction cost), or the existence of some valuable natural resource (accessible, high-quality

33. See Gereffi and Newfarmer, "International Oligopoly."

petroleum, for example) are in a much better bargaining position to maximize concessions from foreign investors than are low-income economies which can offer only low-cost labor. Thus, the advanced economies or those developing countries with high-price minerals can do relatively well in exacting knowledge transfers (or taxes that can pay for knowledge transfers) from multinational corporations eager to gain profits from that location.

Low-income economies with relatively small markets, no high-value resources, and few firm-specific assets competitive with those of MNEs usually have to make large concessions to a multinational to get it to locate there (the multinational generally uses them as a low-cost export platform). The emphasis then becomes cost-reducing concessions—lower taxes, low-cost utilities, and low-cost, docile semiskilled or unskilled labor.

Why make such concessions? The hope is that the multinationals will generate economic growth, creating new demand that will generate increased production of low-technology consumer goods and, gradually, create more physical and human capital for higher-level investments. Although this costs the society implicit and explicit subsidies to the multinationals, the idea is that the presence of "modern" technology production provides learning-by-doing opportunities that other national policies alone could not. In addition, multinationals are viewed as the most efficient form of enterprise (even after taking subsidies into account) capable of delivering modern production locally.

Disadvantages to the Host Economy

Multinationals operate in foreign countries to realize gains on their technology, management skills, marketing capability (access to markets), and access to specialized information that allows them to assess risk and act on that assessment. Their very experience and track record also allow them access to capital that is unavailable to competitors. Taken together, these firm-specific factors are not only difficult to find in domestic firms, but are difficult to acquire in the face of multinational competition. Since such assets are firm-specific, it is also unlikely that multinationals will transfer them willingly to domestic managers and entrepreneurs. Indeed, by engaging in short-term predatory pricing or by denying access to inputs for upstream product development, they may actively attempt to keep domestic firms from competing with them locally. Such policies may be supported by home-base nation-state trade policy as well.

Multinationals are also, on average, not likely to place their highest-return, highest-level activities (requiring the most advanced technology and managerial capacity) on foreign soil. Thus, notes one observer:

> Assets per employee in the parent manufacturing operations of U.S. multinationals were about 20 percent higher than in affiliate operations in developed countries and almost 200 percent higher than in affiliate operations in the developing countries. Similarly compensation per employee in parent operations was about 17 percent higher than in affiliate operations in developed countries and about 360 percent higher than in the developing countries. Although the available data do not show a breakdown of R&D spending by parent and affiliate operations, it is reasonable to expect that the lion's share of R&D by multinationals continues to be done at the parent's location. Given that R&D is a primary source of firm-specific intangible assets and that these assets are hard to manage, most R&D is likely to occur close to home, within the purview of senior management.[34]

This is also the conclusion of a study of MNE behavior in Latin America: "The research and development activities of transnational corporations in developing countries are limited and quite distinct from those in the home countries, using different inputs and/or smaller scales than at home."[35]

34. Tyson, "Does a National Trade Policy Make Sense?" p. 10. This is consistent with the product-cycle theory of direct foreign investment (Raymond Vernon, "International Investment and International Trade in the Product Cycle," *Quarterly Journal of Economics* 80 [June 1966]: 190–207). It argues that the most capital-intensive, technology-intensive, and human-capital-intensive production takes place in those economies with the highest income and highest labor cost (the United States in particular) and that, eventually, as foreign markets grow (as income per capita rises), as new product technology becomes standardized, and as existing products are superseded by even newer models in the most advanced countries, there is an incentive to shift production of the previous generation of technology to other developed countries and, later, to large industrializing countries. More recently others, and even Vernon himself (in the *Oxford Bulletin of Economics and Statistics*, 41, no. 4 [November 1979]: 255–67), have argued that expansionary characteristics of capitalism, such as business cycles, changing markets, and increased competition, are as important as technological change in explaining why firms become MNEs (Gereffi and Newfarmer, "International Oligopoly," p. 394).

Product-cycle theory, however, is still a significant explanation of moves abroad. The equalization of labor costs and income per capita among the developed countries has not altered the power of product-cycle theory to explain the location of multinational production and R&D: the theory predicts that new product development will spread, and it has. Still, the multinationals attempt to locate the most management-intensive, highest-value-added activities close to home under home-base control.

35. Gereffi and Newfarmer, "International Oligopoly," p. 419.

The combination of these factors means that foreign multinationals may displace local firms that, as they developed, would otherwise locate more of their high-value activities as well as more and better jobs locally, with concomitantly greater linkages to local suppliers and additional local technological spillovers. Another result might be greater monopolization of locally produced goods—and hence higher local prices—than would occur in the absence of the multinational.[36]

Not only that, but foreign multinationals may decide, at any moment, in accord with decisions made in corporate offices elsewhere, to shift their distribution of foreign operations or even to close down some activities entirely. Local institutions may have little to say about such decisions. And given foreign firms' limited willingness to transfer key technological and managerial knowledge, not much may be left behind when they do move.

Finally, foreign multinationals may be security risks. The question of how much protection to give domestic suppliers of defense technology is a complex issue, especially when they may not have the latest technology. But the issue is politically important in many larger countries because it symbolizes far wider concerns about sovereignty and technological/economic dependency. Brazil's market reserve policy for smaller computers was adopted primarily for "military security" reasons: the goal was to develop an indigenous computer hardware and software capacity and to become independent from foreign suppliers. Local control of telecommunications networks and technology involves similar issues.

Advantages to the Home Economy

Many of the disadvantages of hosting foreign multinationals are advantages for the nation-state that serves as home base for a multinational. The foreign operations of domestic-based multinationals can enhance profits of the home company, and those profits may be used to increase investment in the expansion of high-value domestic R&D and management-intensive activities. Such foreign operations may also be used to

36. Tyson, "Does a National Trade Policy Make Sense?" p. 24, argues that this is more likely to occur under the following conditions: 1) when the industry is heavily oligopolized to begin with; 2) when the dominant firms in the oligopoly have their home base in a country with lenient antitrust laws; 3) when the industry supplies inputs to a wide range of economic activities; and 4) when the foreign operation is part of the strategy of a foreign, vertically integrated firm to increase market control over a key input in order to gain greater market share in a downstream industry in which profit and technological-development potential are much greater.

acquire new technology, as in the "strategic alliances" of European and Asian domestic production and R&D with U.S. advanced-technology firms.

In today's global economy, domestic multinationals may also be the only sustainable domestic competition for foreign multinationals producing R&D-intensive and capital-intensive goods. This is particularly true in regard to oligopolized products, such as computers, telecommunications, automobiles and other transportation equipment, energy production and distribution, electronics equipment (television, radios, stereos, VCRs), and other consumer durables (e.g., kitchen appliances). Getting access to new technologies may be much cheaper via direct foreign acquisitions than by developing across-the-board R&D activities at home. Conversely, producing in a wider range of markets may be the only way to justify financially a firm's domestic R&D spending and the most effective way to capture the returns on such spending, especially if the firm is using its firm-specific assets to take advantage of oligopoly conditions abroad. This would seem to justify, for example, the Spanish purchase of Chile's telephone network and the attempted purchase of Teléfonos de Mexico (the Southwestern Bell–led group beat out the Spanish offer).

Domestic multinationals are also more likely than foreign multinationals to use domestic sources for local production and to develop through their foreign-affiliate activities the export-marketing infrastructure for other, nonmultinational domestic firms producing other products. In both cases, there may be important "externalities" of domestic multinational operations that do not occur in the case of foreign multinational operations.

Disadvantages to the Home Economy

By definition, multinationals are not only footloose, but also have the managerial capability to develop lower-cost production sites outside a given nation-state. Periodic plant shutdowns are common among multinationals: as labor costs rise locally with economic development, an efficient multinational will systematically move its less management-intensive activities offshore.

The counterargument is that domestic non-MNEs will act similarly, even if through subcontracting, and that this is a logical and efficient result of rising standards of living (i.e., higher wages). A second counterargument is that this is a desirable trend, since the upgrading of jobs and capital input will move the domestic economy into more lucrative, technology-intensive goods and services.

From a distributional standpoint, however, there may be considerable dislocation from such upgrading. Domestic MNE profits will rise, but the wage bill for least-skilled workers will tend to fall, with concomitant consequences for income distribution. The question is whether domestic firms should (or even can) be regulated on such movements, or whether dislocations are better taken care of through a well-thought-out social policy that presumes periodic economic adjustments and job upgrading. Sweden, Japan, and Singapore (with very different political philosophies) have all developed such policy.[37]

DO MULTINATIONAL OPERATIONS DIFFER BY SECTOR?

The largest multinationals are in four sectors: automobiles, petroleum, electronics/high tech, and banking. *Automobile production* can be characterized as a process- or management-intensive industry. *Petroleum* is also management-intensive, but with oligopolized process technology, and is dependent on access to raw materials. Furthermore, ownership of the various segments of petroleum production and distribution can be divided because of the homogeneous nature of the end products. *High-tech industry* is science-based and depends on innovation and learning quickly how to produce new products at low cost (learning by doing). In the present chapter, we will not totally separate producers of electronic goods from producers of semiconductor, computer, and telecommunications goods because, in several cases, a single company makes all these different products. *Banking* is management-intensive, but is concentrated on marketing rather than on production. Some banking technology is developed totally external to the sector (ATMs, computers, telecommunications systems), but other technology—particularly new banking products—is highly internal to financial market management.

Do these features make a significant difference in how multinationals

37. For an account of Swedish economic policy in the 1960s and 1970s, when Sweden promoted increased capital intensity and job upgrading in domestic firms, see Barry Bosworth and Alice Rivlin, *The Swedish Economy* (Washington, D.C.: Brookings, 1987); see also Martin Carnoy and Derek Shearer, *Economic Democracy* (Armonk, N.Y.: M. E. Sharpe, 1980).

operate in each sector? And what does this mean for nation-state policies toward MNEs in each sector?

The Automobile Industry

Auto production has been multinational for at least sixty years. Both Ford and GM had plants in Germany and Japan in the 1920s, and they reestablished operations in Germany after World War II. FIAT built plants in Spain, Yugoslavia, Poland, and the Soviet Union in the 1950s and 1960s. U.S. and European companies (Volkswagen was among the most active) also established production in Latin America (in Argentina, Brazil, Mexico, and Venezuela) as part of that region's import-substitution policy (Ford had built an assembly plant in Mexico as early as 1925). All these plants operated in separate markets and were largely self-contained production units; although so long as models matched home-country production and so long as content requirements did not interfere, parts continued to be exported to the periphery. The driving force behind multinationalism was protective tariffs, avoiding high transportation costs (relative to sales price), and exploiting specific firm assets in mass production—this in a period of rapid oligopolization of the world auto industry.

To a great extent, protective tariffs and specific firm assets still explain multinationalism today, but the auto industry itself has changed radically and, with it, the nature of multinationalism.

(1) As the demand for automobiles expanded worldwide, the possibilities for product differentiation also increased. The Japanese, before anyone else, understood that through parts standardization and modularization, economies of scale in the stamping, or body-style, phase of production could be forgone. Profits could come by way of increased sales from greater body-style differentiation. The Japanese also introduced much higher quality-control standards. They simultaneously increased assembly-line productivity through innovative (peculiarly Japanese) management techniques and—in a world marked by increasing repair costs and the increasing cost of time—were also able to sell product reliability and customer service.

With economies of scale transferred to standardized and modularized parts, runs of 100,000 of a single body style (in low-price models; even fewer in higher-priced ones), when assembled at a single location, could be profitable. An automaker could buy a standardized part for all models from a single supplier or build a huge engine plant in one low-cost labor location and then use those engines over many years, with a series of modifications, in many different body types.

(2) Marketing and design have become much more important and complex operations in the auto industry because of greatly increased market differentiation. Today, because of the high price of an automobile, repair rates and customer service are crucial factors in one's marketing strategy, which means that producers have to develop even greater marketing coordination among dealerships than they had to in the past. And with increased competition—Japanese automakers are aggressively attempting to move into every national market, with products ranging from low-end economy cars to luxury sedans—the time required to bring new designs and technical innovations into the marketplace has been sharply reduced.

(3) With increased competition, management of the auto plants themselves has also become more complex. Parts are coming from distant plants, and controls on quality and inventory accumulation are much tighter. The most successful auto companies are those which are best able to develop their market strategies and to maintain low rates of error that, in turn, imply new management techniques on the shop floor.

(4) The key role of product design and quality control as a way of winning a greater share of diverse markets, together with the increased cost of innovative activities, is also dispersing the industry's R&D. Thus, "The profusion of technological choice and escalation of research costs . . . have prompted companies to externalize research, increase joint ventures in design and development of new products and processes, and decentralize research and design functions."[38]

Figures 3.4 and 3.5 show that, between 1987 and 1990, the world's major automakers increasingly entered into business arrangements with each other, both in developed and in developing countries, in order to a) share the costs of research and development while competing in production, marketing, and servicing of product; b) trade components; c) produce or assemble components jointly; or d) market products jointly. Multinational auto firms, therefore, are increasingly subcontracting not just parts production but even engineering and design: "Under these arrangements, suppliers are not only participants in research, design, and development,

---

38. Rebecca Morales and Carlos Quandt, "The New Regionalism: Developing Countries and Regional Collaborative Competition," *International Journal of Urban and Regional Research* (Oxford) (September 1992).

Figure 3.4. Interrelationships among the world's major automakers, developed countries only, 1987–1990.

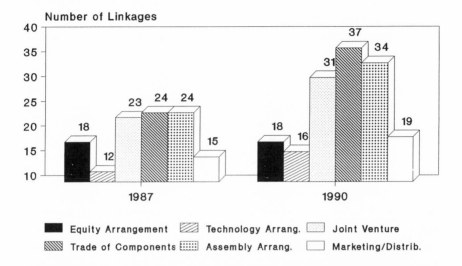

SOURCE: *WARD's Automotive International;* reproduced, by permission, from Rebecca Morales and Carlos Quandt, "The New Regionalism: Developing Countries and Regional Collaborative Competition," *International Journal of Urban and Regional Research* (Oxford) (September 1992).

but increasingly survive by continually strengthening their R&D capability."[39]

(5) The increased intensity of R&D and the greater focus on quality control should logically have led auto production to relocate "back North," as some analysts predicted even a few years ago.[40] But major multinational producers have instead employed a successful strategy of decentralizing even management-intensive processes to developing countries. Focusing on labor and on management-training programs has enabled them to take advantage of low-cost labor without giving up quality or productivity. For example, Ford's most productive engine and stamping/final assembly plants in North America are

39. Ibid., p. 6.
40. See Juan Rada, "Information Technology and the Third World," in Tom Forester (ed.), *The Information Technology Revolution* (Cambridge: MIT Press, 1985); Gerd Junne, "Automation in the North: Consequences for Developing Countries' Exports," in James R. Caporaso (ed.), *A Changing International Division of Labor* (Boulder: Lynne Rienner, 1987); and Peter Drucker, "The Changing World Economy," *Foreign Affairs* 64, no. 4 (Spring 1986): 768–91.

Figure 3.5. Interrelationships among the world's major automakers, developed countries and developing countries, 1987–1990.

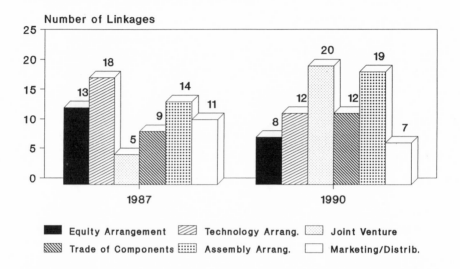

SOURCE: *WARD's Automotive International*; reproduced, by permission, from Rebecca Morales and Carlos Quandt, "The New Regionalism: Developing Countries and Regional Collaborative Competition," *International Journal of Urban and Regional Research* (Oxford) (September 1992).

in Chihuahua and Hermosillo, Mexico. Both plants are physical-capital-intensive *and* human-capital-intensive. Moreover, the Hermosillo plant was built in cooperation with a Japanese manufacturing-equipment firm, its major parts suppliers are also Japanese, and it has Mexican managers successfully using many of the Japanese management techniques.[41] Output of both plants is entirely destined for the U.S. market.

(6) In the past fifteen years, some auto producers have seen their principal locus of profit shift away from the home-base country to foreign subsidiaries. This is certainly the case for Ford, which increasingly depends on its European operations as a profit center,[42] Volkswagen's largest

41. See Shaiken, *Mexico in the Global Economy*. Shaiken discusses only the Hermosillo plant in this book, but most of what he says also applies to the engine assembly plant in Chihuahua.

42. Since 1979, Ford Europe has earned equal or higher profits in comparison with its North American parent in five of ten years, on sales that average about 25 percent of North America's. Even so, European profits are not nearly large enough to sustain Ford's R&D efforts, located principally in the United States. See "Can Europe Save Ford's Future—Again?" *New York Times*, October 28, 1990.

production location is not Germany, but Brazil, and Honda has shifted almost 50 percent of its production and much of its profits over the past eight years to the United States. In this sense, the auto industry is becoming *increasingly global*, losing its national profit-center identity.[43]

(7) The greatest pressure on automobile firms to become global, however, is still protectionism—the power of national political aims imposing themselves on comparative prices. In the current phase of the international political economy, this manifests itself increasingly in regional terms, with the big markets—Europe, North America, and Japan—defending themselves against each other's imports. The United States has long had plants in Europe, and the Europeans have tried, somewhat unsuccessfully, to build plants in the United States. Now the Japanese are entering Europe through the United Kingdom after successful ventures in the United States. Although the original Japanese production operations in the United States (Honda) came before the quotas, it was quotas that spurred Honda sales and brought in other producers.

The present phase is having another important effect on MNE globalism: buying national versus foreign-made automobiles is increasingly becoming a political statement on the part of the consumer, and that puts pressure on foreign multinationals *to take on local national identities*. For example, a number of imported Honda models sold in the United States are called Acura, and Honda operations in the United States are now referred to as American Honda. Honda is making a concerted effort to be viewed in the United States as an *American* company, not only to avert consumer backlash but to gain entrance into European markets by shipping from the United States. Honda's "Americanness" (in Honda's view) will be achieved by gradually increasing the percentage of American Honda's officers who are Americans (50 percent currently) and by moving an increased proportion of its R&D to the United States. Simultaneously, Honda is opening an independent plant in Britain to compete directly with Toyota and Nissan on European soil.[44] Again, Japanese automakers are trying hard to blend into the European countryside in order to lessen nationalist backlash. Local production as an alternative to exports from the home base contributes to such "blending in," for the foreign firm can lay some claim to being a local employer, helping bring economic growth and technological development to the local economy.

43. See United Nations Centre on Transnational Corporations, *Transnational Corporations in the International Auto Industry* (New York: United Nations, 1983).

44. Interview with Tetsuo Chino, former president of American Honda, November 7, 1990.

(8) Yet, despite these attempts at achieving a global *image*, and even some movement toward real globality, auto multinationals retain the lion's share of their R&D at home. (Ninety percent of Honda's R&D remains in Japan, as does nearly 100 percent of the production for the most R&D-intensive parts—the electronic components—used in their U.S.-made autos; Ford's R&D, too, remains almost entirely in the United States.) Moreover, *strategic decisions are made at the home base.* This is true even when a high percentage of profits are earned abroad. The role of foreign automaker operations, in this sense, is still that of a subsidiary. But host nation-states do have the potential power to negotiate how much of the management decisionmaking and participation in innovative activities will take place outside the home base.

The Petroleum Industry

Declining petroleum prices in the 1980s, the absence of any "big" oil finds, and the high capital-investment cost of building new refineries produced a major restructuring in the petroleum industry during the decade.

(1) OPEC oil producers, such as Kuwait, Saudi Arabia, and Venezuela, themselves became major multinationals by purchasing "downstream" refining capacity and gasoline sales networks, mainly in Europe. The Saudis have also almost taken over the entire operation of ARAMCO, the old consortium of Western oil companies' holdings in the oil kingdoms. Such purchases and management takeovers were undertaken mainly to ensure markets for their crude oil in what was increasingly a buyer's market, but it also gives greater control to the crude oil producers at the more technologically advanced end of the industry. At the same time, downstream operations had become the more profitable part of the petroleum business. According to Standard & Poor's:

> The move downstream is in part a natural evolution, in which producing countries move from the development of domestic refining and marketing capacity—largely to reduce their reliance on foreign oil companies—to the construction of export refineries in the late seventies, and, ultimately, to acquiring offshore refining and marketing assets. The encroachment of producer countries into the traditional downstream markets of the major companies in many instances reflected a mutuality of interests: producer coun-

tries were looking for secure outlets for their crude, while the majors were pulling out of marginal areas attractive to producer countries with downstream aspirations.[45]

Kuwait, for example, took over Gulf's European marketing and distribution network in 1984 and, more recently, acquired RTZ's Spanish refining interests. In 1986, the Venezuelan national oil company acquired 50 percent of Southland's Citgo refinery and marketing operations; in 1988, the Saudis purchased a 50 percent stake in Texaco's eastern and Gulf Coast refining and marketing operations (11,000 brand-name stations); and Abu Dhabi now holds an 8.5 percent stake of France's CFP. Non-OPEC producers also moved downstream: Norway (Statoil) bought Exxon's Scandinavian assets; Mexico took over 34 percent of a Spanish refinery, Petronur.

The refiner also profits from vertical *re*integration,[46] which guarantees a permanent commitment of crude reserves to its markets. Even integrated operators have to buy substantial portions of their crude oil requirements to feed their refineries. In a typical deal, the foreign producer makes a single cash payment to the refiner and agrees to supply one-half of the crude oil requirements in exchange for half the net revenues at the highest marketing level the deal includes. But some deals, such as the one with Kuwait or Norway, entail full ownership and operation of refining and marketing by the purchasing producer.

(2) Environmental concerns in the largest single market, the United States, and in Europe—concerns about new drilling, new refinery capacity, and pollutants in gasoline and other petroleum products—are leading to greater concentration of refining and marketing as firms unable to cope with potential supply shortages and the increased costs of refining are purchased by other firms moving to eliminate competition, to gain access to crude oil, and to secure particular markets. The recent purchase of Mobil's Ferndale, Washington, refinery and its West Coast service stations by British Petroleum's Sohio division (which pumps Alaska crude) is part of this concentration process. Mobil has responded by buying Tenneco's Louisiana refinery and Sohio's service station network on the East Coast. Even more significant, eleven of America's twenty-five largest indepen-

45. Standard & Poor's, *Industry Surveys* (Oil), August 3, 1989, p. O-26.

46. For some companies, such as Texaco, which controlled significant shares of Persian Gulf oil up to the 1970s, the purchase of their downstream operations means a return to pre-1970s integration but *under producer-country ownership*.

dent oil and gas companies in 1980 have been acquired, merged, or sold off.

(3) Whereas oil-producing countries are acquiring downstream operations, importers are moving upstream to control access to crude. The extreme case of imported fuel dependence is Japan. Because of concern over the nation's almost exclusive reliance on imported oil, Japan's Ministry for International Trade and Industry (MITI), notes Standard & Poor's, "has launched a program to increase the proportion of Japanese-owned oil in imports to 30 percent from its current 12 percent. The Japanese have entered approximately a dozen upstream ventures in the U.S., including partnerships with Texaco, Chevron, Conoco, Arco, and Amoco, and are also entering joint ventures in Asia and Europe. The [Japanese] government may also sweeten the pot with credits or premium depreciation rates for companies involved in foreign E&P [exploration and production]."[47]

Just as important, Japan is following the French strategy of building nuclear plants that will greatly reduce its oil dependence. Nuclear power generation is targeted to provide 50 percent of Japan's energy supply over the next twenty years. Thanks to government incentives, industry standardization, and the absence of costly courtroom and regulatory delays, the Japanese can reportedly build a nuclear plant "twice as fast and at half the cost of its typical American counterpart."[48]

(4) As developing-country crude oil producers have moved downstream into refining, integrated petrochemical companies in the developed countries are moving horizontally into other forms of energy and farther downstream into biotechnology. The large oil companies are therefore no longer just oil companies—they have large stakes in nuclear energy, coal, and alternative forms of energy, including the use of biomass and its conversion to biogas or fuel alcohol. Their interest in biotechnology goes beyond alternative fuels, however: biotechnology can be used to produce polymers that would help make it possible for more oil to be pumped to the wells; it may enable new products to be developed using oil and gas; and, since oil companies such as Shell are also agrochemical companies,

47. Standard & Poor's, *Industry Surveys* (Oil), August 3, 1989, p. O-34. The largest Japanese oil companies (Nippon Oil and Idemitsu Kosan) are small compared to such huge multinationals as Exxon, with about 30 percent of Exxon's sales but only 6 percent of its profit in 1989 (see *Fortune*, July 30, 1990).

48. Standard & Poor's, *Industry Surveys* (Oil), August 3, 1989, p. O-35.

they share the same interest in biotechnology as other chemical companies.[49]

(5) The opening of the former Soviet Union and China to Western petroleum technology could make them increasingly important oil players in the 1990s and beyond. Currently, the former USSR has about 16 percent of the world's oil-refining capacity, and China another 2.4 percent. This makes the former Soviet Union the world's largest (and probably most inefficient) oil and gas producer, and China the largest oil exporter in Asia. Both badly need foreign technology, however, if they can hope to expand production significantly. With this in mind, they are pursuing joint-venture arrangements with foreign manufacturers of oil field equipment, refiners, and petrochemical companies. Chevron, for example, is about to begin oil and gas exploration in the former USSR. This provides enormous possibilities for foreign multinationals to break into an important new market; and more efficient production (and new oil finds) spurred by new technology could provide the former Soviets and the Chinese with a significant source of foreign exchange to finance other badly needed investments.

High Technology

More than any other industry, the manufacture of semiconductors, computers, and telecommunication products is at the core of the information revolution. It is especially significant, then, that semiconductor and computer production are especially globalized, with even small Silicon Valley firms entering into international strategic alliances with other firms, both domestic-based and foreign.[50] Yet, despite continued innovation within small firms, the industry is dominated by vertically integrated giants such as IBM, Matsushita, General Electric, Philips, NEC, Siemens, Mitsubishi, Toshiba, DEC, and Thomson.

Fifteen or even ten years ago, high tech was totally dominated by U.S. firms and U.S. products. The United States dominated the semiconductor

49. Rob Van Tulder and Gerd Junne, *European Multinationals in Core Technologies* (New York: John Wiley, 1988), p. 59.

50. See Richard Gordon, "Markets, Hierarchies, and Alliances: Beyond the Flexible Specialization Debate," Silicon Valley Research Group, University of California–Santa Cruz, 1990 (mimeo.).

(chip) market, computer products, software, and even telecommunications technology. This has changed radically.

(1) The Japanese have quickly come to dominate the high-volume integrated circuit (IC) market and, with that, are also beginning to gain an increasing share of the semiconductor capital equipment industry (40 percent in 1987). The United States still leads in the design of complex microprocessor chips and application-specific integrated circuits (ASICs); but in large dynamic random-access memory chips (DRAMs), where Japanese companies now have more than 90 percent of the market, all U.S. companies except IBM have practically given up competing individually. IBM continues to make its own memory chips and to develop next-generation memories.[51]

Because semiconductors are the "core of the core" of the microelectronics cluster and are vital inputs into many end products, a national presence in such production is considered crucial for maintaining a competitive advantage in downstream high-technology products. Both the U.S. and the European answer to Japanese dominance of high-volume memory chip production has been R&D consortia: Siemens, Philips, and Thomson formed JESSI; and U.S. semiconductor producers, under the leadership of National Semiconductor's Charles Sporck, have formed Sematech. Both consortia have considerable government funding. In addition, there has been a continuous move toward vertical integration of chip production into large multiproduct electronic firms (such as IBM) in order to facilitate control of supply.[52]

(2) In computers, IBM continues to dominate the worldwide market. Its $63 billion in sales and $4 billion in profits for 1989 far surpassed NEC's and Fujitsu's (IBM's chief competitors in Japan). Indeed, IBM's profits were eight times greater than what NEC and Fujitsu earned from the production of *all* products—computers and noncomputers. IBM is a very globalized company, but so are all the players in this market: even the "smaller" companies, such as Apple, Compaq, and Sun, have most of their components built outside the United States. Macro- as well as minicomputer firms (e.g., DEC and Hewlett-Packard) source their components abroad and earn a significant share of profits from foreign assembly and sales.

Leader IBM has recently undergone organizational changes in order to

51. Jeffrey Bairstow, "Can the U.S. Semiconductor Industry Be Saved," *High Technology* 7, no. 5 (May 1987): 34–40.

52. Ibid., p. 38. See also Van Tulder and Junne, *European Multinationals*, pp. 33–39.

meet more intensive competition, but its overall shape as a company is basically unchanged. Mainframe sales still deliver from 70 to 75 percent of the company's profits. It is still a truly global company, with almost 60 percent of its sales and 75 percent of its profits in 1988 coming from overseas. Eight billion dollars in sales come from Japan alone, where it is number three, behind NEC and Fujitsu. There, IBM introduced a laptop computer with full Japanese-language capability as early as 1987 while U.S. customers still waited for one. The company has research labs in England, France, Japan, and Germany.

As a major player so heavily dependent on foreign operations, IBM has been particularly sensitive to its "foreignness" and has attempted to maintain a domestic "protective coloration" in each country—at least in Europe, Japan, and the smaller Canadian and Australian markets. Its labs, production plants, and sales offices abroad are almost entirely staffed by locals. Thus, the president of IBM Japan is Takeo Shiina. In a recent response to Europe's 1992 regionalization, the Paris regional office was closed and more local autonomy was given to its individual country operations.[53] In this sense, IBM serves as a model for Japanese and European companies attempting to keep anti-foreign-multinational feelings from adversely affecting operations and products abroad.[54]

Yet, IBM's product strategy, organizational decisions, financial decisions, and the bulk of its R&D stay very much in the United States. The firm has invested in a number of software companies (mostly U.S.-based) and has joined a consortium of investors in U.S. Memories, a company that aims to reduce U.S. dependence on Japan for DRAM. Moreover, IBM announced in 1990 that it was producing a U.S.-developed, 4-megabit memory device in large volume, putting it well ahead of its competitors. Its mainframe R&D as well as its mainframe networking R&D, the principal sources of IBM's profits, are all U.S.-based.

Furthermore, IBM's behavior in such less-developed countries (LDCs) as Mexico and Brazil is not nearly so sensitive to local sentiment. These are essentially assembly and sales operations (most of the components are imported from IBM production operations in the Far East) involving little or no technology transfer and incorporating considerable political interference in an attempt to influence overall national technology policy.

53. Interview with Eugene Creighton, IBM World Trade Americas Group, Tarrytown, New York, November 6, 1990; interview with Gerard Compain, Bull Corporation, Paris, October 10, 1990.
54. Interview with Tetsuo Chino, former president of American Honda, November 7, 1990.

However, it is difficult even for European companies to compete with IBM, especially in its bread-and-butter mainframe business. For example, Philips, Siemens, and Bull tried to develop their own mainframe models in the UNIDATA project during the 1970s but failed when Bull went in with Honeywell (see Table 3.3). The alternative was to develop IBM-plug-compatible equipment, using Japanese mainframes, and to specialize in midsize and personal computers. This European companies have done with some success.[55] It is in these areas that European and now Japanese companies have followed IBM's lead in developing strategic alliances with small, innovative firms (usually U.S.) that can help the larger multinational gain some comparative advantage in one or another niche of the market. These alliances are often assisted or even stimulated by government intervention (for European examples, see Table 3.3).

(3) In telecommunications, markets are much more national and "national champions" much more successful in competing with the more globalized producers like ATT. Even ATT, though, is largely U.S.-national. Below, we analyze the national champion phenomenon in more detail. Because of national standards and the importance of national control of infrastructure, it is evident that telecommunications is likely always to be more localized than semiconductors or computers. However, this set of high-tech products is also especially marked by strategic alliances between national champions and foreign firms having R&D capacity in certain niches of the telecommunications market. Furthermore, it is also in this area that international alliances are being made to take over LDC telecommunications systems. The recent bidding on Telemex, the Mexican telephone system, is a good example of this trend.[56]

The Banking Sector

International banking has gone through major changes in the past ten years, led by deregulation/liberalization, increased globalization, and the ascendancy of Japanese banking.

(1) Between 1979 and the mid-1980s, most industrialized economies eliminated foreign-exchange controls and deregulated domestic banking, first in the United States (1980–81) and then in the United Kingdom and Japan (1986–87). The catalysts for reform varied by country. In the

---

55. Van Tulder and Junne, *European Multinationals*, pp. 41–42.
56. *New York Times*, November 16, 1990.

United States, reform was pushed by an expansionist banking system; in Japan, expanding government debt, owing largely to the oil crisis of the late 1970s, was the catalyst.[57] The British government initiated reforms in a financial sector it felt was too restrictive: liberalization was seen as a way to increase competition among the big financial corporations, stimulating the British economy and the stock market. The strategy was largely successful.[58]

Deregulation in these key markets has allowed the world's major financial institutions to move funds freely across borders and among currencies. Although large multinational banks, such as Citicorp (previously First National City Bank) and Bank of America, had established affiliates and owned large blocks of shares in foreign banks by the 1960s, deregulation allowed a massive expansion of international banking. More banks were able to operate on a multinational level, opening branches abroad, financing corporate leveraged buyouts in foreign countries, buying foreign firms, and so forth. New financial products were also created out of deregulation: Eurocurrencies, Eurobonds, offshore bond trading, floating interest rates, Euroequity issues, and junk bonds. In addition, there has been a tremendous increase in the role played by nonbanking financial institutions, such as securities companies, holding companies, consortia, and insurance companies, in international financial markets.

(2) The late 1970s and early 1980s also saw the growth of major new sources of venture-capital financing, and these have begun to move worldwide through specialized mutual funds. For example, the largest U.S. funding sources for industrial investments today are General Electric Finance and Westinghouse Finance, which grew out of tax shelter strategies in the early 1980s. General Electric Finance alone has more than $80 billion in assets, one-third those of Citicorp, the largest U.S. commercial bank.

(3) At the same time, international finance has become computerized and hooked into worldwide telecommunications networks. Many financial institutions have twenty-four-hour trading capabilities, and large institutional investors engage in automatic ("program") computerized trading, often worldwide, and in diverse financial instruments. As a result, markets

---

57. See Thomas F. Cargill and Shoichi Royama, *The Transition of Finance in Japan and the United States*.

58. See Sarkis Khoury and Alo Ghosh, *Recent Developments in International Banking and Finance*, vol. 1 (Lexington, Mass.: D. C. Heath, 1987).

Table 3.3. Major Structural Changes and Government Intervention in the Electronics Industry in France, Germany, and the United Kingdom, 1968–1984.

FRANCE

1968	1970	1973	1975	1978	1978–79	1981–82	1983–84
Government fosters SECO (Thomson) and COSEM (CSF) merger to create SECOSEM (Thomson), heavily supported by state	EFCIS (semiconductors) created as joint venture between Thomson and CEA (Atomic Energy Commission)	Creation of UNIDATA (computers), a joint venture of CII, Siemens, and Philips. Uncertain government attitude	Failure of UNIDATA. Government supports merger of CII and Honeywell-Bull	Thomson takes over semiconductor division of LTT and SILEC	Government supports joint ventures of: Saint-Gobain/National Semiconductor; Matra/Harris; Thomson/Motorola. Saint-Gobain entry into CII and Olivetti. Support of Radio-Technique (Philips). Now 5 poles of production	Nationalization of CGE, Thomson, Saint-Gobain, CII-HB (becomes Bull); majority stake in Matra	Concentration of computer activities of Thomson, Saint-Gobain, and CGE with Bull. Thomson takes over the joint venture of Saint-Gobain and National Semiconductor (Eurotechnique) and the semiconductor business of CGE. Of the 5 poles of production, only 2 remain. Saint-Gobain withdraws from Olivetti, CGE takes a 10% share in the Italian firm

GERMANY

1970	1973	1975	1978–79	1979–80	1983	1984
Creation of DA-TEL. Joint venture of state, Siemens, AEG-Telefunken, Nixdorf (in computer applications)	Creation of UNIDATA (see above). Favorable government attitude	Siemens takes over big computer division of AEG (approved by state)	Rescue of AEG-Telefunken by a consortium of banks. Indirect federal support	Plans for the establishment of a joint research laboratory of the three major firms and public agencies (Berlin Synchrotron Projekt)	Semiconductor division of AEG merged with Mostek (United Technologies) in a joint venture. Telefunken taken over by Thomson	Joint research in Germany of ICL, Siemens, and Bull (in computers and information technology). Takeover of Grundig by Philips (after disapproval by the Bundeskartelamt of the same effort by Thomson)

U.K.

1968	1976–78	1978	1980	1984
Joint venture between Mullard (Philips) and GEC, taken over by the former. Series of mergers lead to ICL (computers), 10.5% owned by state	NEB buys shares in Ferranti (computers, semiconductors, military, etc.) and in various small and medium firms in software, industrial and consumer electronics	Constitution by NEB of INMOS (VLSI memories and MPUs). Entirely publicly financed	Conservative government sells ICL and Ferranti to private market	Government sells its 75% share in INMOS to Thorn-EMI. STC (25% owned by ITT) tries to acquire ICL

SOURCE: Reproduced by permission from Rob Van Tulder and Gerd Junne, *European Multinationals in Core Technologies* (John Wiley, 1988), table 6.1.

NOTE: VLSI = very large-scale integration; MPUs = microprocessor units have become more interdependent and interlocked, and international finance has become much more volatile.

(4) The rise in Japanese banking was made possible mainly by domestic deregulation policies, which allowed mergers of already large banks such as Mitsui and Taiyo Kobe (1989) and turned them into global giants, and by U.S. deregulation policies, which gave Japanese banks access to growing financial markets on the West Coast that was not available to U.S. banks chartered in other states, such as Citicorp and Chase Manhattan, until 1991.[59]

In addition, Japanese strategy, both in the United States and Europe, appears to be different from that of U.S. and European banks: the Japanese tend to concentrate more on merchant and commercial lending, principally to middle-market businesses. The advantage of this strategy lies in gaining access to the corporate client base of domestic financial institutions and in providing entry for the Japanese banks' industrial clients into foreign markets. The linkage between Japanese banks and their domestic clients is unusually strong.[60] In 1987, 30 percent of the asset portfolios of Japanese banks were in business loans, compared with 19.5 percent for U.S. banks. In Europe, they are pursuing the same strategy. In July 1989, Taiyo Kobe Bank announced its intent to buy a 5 percent share in a subsidiary of Italy's Credito Commerciale. In this way, Taiyo Kobe hopes to use its association with Credito Commerciale to identify joint-venture prospects in southern Europe for its many medium-size company clients in Japan.[61] And whereas Japanese banks have reached into deregulated foreign markets, they have prohibited (or at least made very difficult) entry by foreign banks into their own market.

(5) The decline of U.S. banking derives from the failure of its high-risk loan strategy in developing countries during the 1970s and in domestic real estate during the deregulated 1980s. U.S. banks have also placed

59. Thus, Japanese banks have recently purchased the Bank of California and have opened branches of Japanese banks in California (Sanwa Bank, Sumutomo Bank, and others). See "Japanese Establish a West Coast Foothold: A Golden Opportunity," *Far Eastern Economic Review*, March 1989, pp. 81–82.

60. Therese Flaherty and Itami Hiroyuki, "The Banking-Industrial Complex," in Daniel Okimoto and Thomas Rohlen (eds.), *Inside the Japanese System* (Stanford: Stanford University Press, 1988), pp. 54–56. "In Japan, the relationships among the city banks and the two-way relations between firms and their lead banks amount to a virtual 'banking-industrial complex.' . . . The dealings between the banks and the firms in this complex are not arm's-length transactions" (p. 54).

61. "Japanese Bank Joins Nomura in Southern Europe," *Far Eastern Economic Review*, August 1989, p. 55.

considerable emphasis on consumer and real estate loans worldwide. Such retail banking concentrates on home loans, car loans, and credit card services. For example, Citicorp, the largest foreign bank in the Far East, uses its branches in foreign countries as "deployment centers" for bank representatives who drum up business from real estate agents and car dealers. It has also launched an intensive advertising campaign for its three credit cards and has been trying to tap into the high-end consumer market by negotiating deals with art auction houses and luxury boat retailers.[62]

More than in other sectors, then, multinational strategies are highly influenced by the local corporate financial culture. In Japan, banks are characteristically wed to industrial clients; hence, they have made themselves joint-venture or acquisition middlemen worldwide. U.S. banks have moved heavily into consumer credit and out of industrial investment domestically, and so have pursued that same strategy globally. Industrial investing in the United States is increasingly the domain of specialized industrial investors. European banks are now concentrating even more on Europe than they have in the past because of the move to join European markets and currencies in the early 1990s. European banks are also very active in their home countries' former colonies. And all the banks are highly affected by domestic economic conditions, no matter how extensive their global activities.

WHICH COUNTRY'S FOREIGN MULTINATIONAL, AND DOES IT MATTER?

Multinational corporations choose to invest in a particular country on the basis of their own market advantage in that country, the size of the country's market for their products, the degree to which the country protects against imports, and the degree to which the country protects against foreign investment. Some economies, such as the U.S. economy, have traditionally focused on trade policy and have let foreign investors enter their markets almost without restriction. The United Kingdom has also been an economy open to foreign investment, and despite greater

---

62. "Citicorp Targets Asia's New Consumer Power: Streetwise Strategy," *Far Eastern Economic Review*, March 1990, p. 38.

restrictions on foreign investments in continental Europe, non-European foreign firms (primarily U.S.) have a significant stake in the continent's economy, especially in the technologically advanced sectors.

But the spectacular rise of the Japanese economy, notably its globalization in the form of increased influence over international finance, trade, and direct foreign investment, has changed the attitude that many once had concerning free access to foreign MNEs. A rapid influx of Japanese capital into the United States has sparked widespread debate.[63] The majority of Americans now support restrictions on Japanese investment.[64] A similar debate is under way in Europe.[65]

Are there significant differences between Japanese and European/U.S. multinationals such that economies should prefer foreign investments from Europeans and Americans rather than from the Japanese? Briefly, we can summarize the arguments in the following way.

(1) In one analyst's words, "We do not yet live in the age of the 'global corporation,' nor, in its logical concomitant, a world of politically undifferentiated economic spaces."[66] As we have shown, multinationals tend to keep most of their assets and sales in their home-base country, and their foreign affiliates behave very much in step with the strategies and management style developed at the home base; and these, in turn, are influenced by the economic conditions and constraints on corporate behavior at home. Furthermore, multinationals often take orders from their home governments (especially when an investment or production decision affects "national interests") and are often helped in gaining a better position by their government's intervention.[67]

(2) Multinationals from different countries *do* appear to behave differently. For example, French companies investing in industrial countries, because they are relative latecomers, are more likely to acquire or participate in existing companies. They are also likely to maintain much of the

---

63. See, for example, Tyson, "Does a National Trade Policy Make Sense?"; Cohen, "Testimony." Also see *Fortune*, January 29, February 12, and February 26, 1990.

64. Lee Smith, "Fear and Loathing of Japan," *Fortune*, February 26, 1990, p. 51.

65. Shawn Tully, "Now Japan's Autos Push into Europe," *Fortune*, January 29, 1990, p. 96.

66. Cohen, "Testimony," p. 2.

67. Cohen (ibid.) cites the examples of U.S. corporations' unwillingness to cooperate in de Gaulle's *Force de Frappe* project, causing its subsequent failure, and the reaction of U.S.-based MNEs' to the Soviet-European pipeline. There are many other examples, notably the U.S. government's tight policy on technology transfer and its interventions in other countries' domestic policies regarding direct foreign investment—the IBM case in Mexico for one—and the enormous pressure put on Brazil to eliminate its market reserve policy in micro- and minicomputers.

existing management structure intact, since they are primarily interested in market penetration or in acquiring a particular, complementary technology (strategic alliance) and do not (in those countries) have a generalizable comparative advantage in management technique.

U.S. MNEs, long-time players in the international economy, are also likely to hire a high percentage of local managers. In one study of U.S. and Japanese multinationals in the United Kingdom, John Dunning found that at similar stages of their entry into the British market, the U.S. companies had a significantly higher percentage of British managers.[68] Companies such as IBM and U.S. automakers have learned to keep a "country friendly" profile in Europe and Japan by "indigenizing" local affiliates so that they take on the character of domestic producers.

Japanese firms tend to export management style, since this is in large part what makes them more competitive than U.S. and European firms. This necessarily makes them distinctly Japanese, at once an advantage (their management style is admired for its efficiency and "equality") but also a disadvantage, since it requires a greater percentage of Japanese managers for a longer period of time and, concomitantly, a greater degree of control by those who are totally versed in the parent company's management philosophy. Nevertheless, Japanese MNEs are under increasing pressure to "melt into the countryside."

They also tend to operate in ways that favor other Japanese companies in complementary sectors and in other, nonrelated sectors—more so than U.S. MNEs coordinating their policies with other American firms. This is largely a function of the intensive network of MNEs in Japan and the close relationships between its banks and industrial companies.[69] Even as they compete intensively within the same sector, they are more likely to count on Japanese firms for their inputs and, in the case of banks, to use their affiliates to promote Japanese firms in foreign markets. Thus, Japanese automakers in the United States still buy only 67 percent of their inputs in the United States, the rest coming from Japan.[70] And, as mentioned above, a high percentage of the Japanese banking business worldwide consists of lending to Japanese firms doing business abroad. The Japanese

68. John Dunning, *Decision-making Structure in United States and Japanese Manufacturing Affiliates in the United Kingdom: Some Similarities and Contrasts*, Working Paper no. 41 (Geneva: ILO, Multinational Enterprise Programme, 1986).

69. See, for example, James C. Abegglen and George Stalk, Jr., *Kaisha: The Japanese Corporation* (New York: Basic Books, 1985).

70. *Fortune*, February 27, 1990, p. 53.

import trade is also dominated by Japanese multinationals, again more so than in other countries: in 1986, for example, intrafirm trade "accounted for 48.5 percent of U.S. exports to Europe compared to 72 percent of U.S. exports to Japan. . . . Japan's import trade, as well as its export trade is conducted to a distinctly large extent by Japanese multinationals. This is not the case for either the U.S. or Europe."[71]

(3) Multinationals from various countries are also more or less nationalistic because of a tendency to be closely or distantly related to their national states. U.S. and British MNEs, perhaps more than any other country's, are philosophically antistate and therefore tend to be more "footloose." Even though they are highly "American" or "British," especially when they need government help in securing economic interests, they are also first and foremost profitmaking private enterprises, obligated to their (international) stockholders, not to any nation-state.

This is not nearly as true for continental European or Japanese corporations. For one thing, some of the largest European MNEs are state-owned. Also, even when, as in the case of France, the MNEs are not state-owned, their multinationalization has come about through specific state policies of industrial concentration, whose principal aim was to give the companies of the home country "a 'foothold on the international ladder' and counter foreign competition."[72] In the Japanese case, government export-oriented policies were instrumental in ultimately pushing private companies in particular directions, first multinationalizing into lower-income countries in Asia to reduce the labor costs of more traditional products, then increasing the technology content of exports, and then rapidly increasing foreign direct investments in industrial countries, largely to get around protective quotas.[73] At one time (1975) the Japanese government was insisting on investments in enterprises that directly bolstered industry at home. For example, when Matsushita Electric acquired Motorola's TV-production facilities in America, it did so to enlarge its modest share of the U.S. market, but simultaneously it brought in machinery and product components made in Japan.[74]

Although Japanese (and certain European) MNEs may not be state-owned, they tend to be "state-tied"—that is, their operations may be

71. Tyson, "Does a National Trade Policy Make Sense?" p. 28.

72. Michalet and Chevalier, "France," p. 91.

73. Ozawa, "Japan."

74. Louis Kraar, "The Japanese Are Coming—With Their Own Style of Management," *Fortune*, March 1975, pp. 116–21.

shaped by powerful state policies that allow them to gain advantages over host-country firms and other MNEs. Part of this advantage lies in liberal antitrust policies in Japan and Europe that allow for close horizontal cooperation between domestic firms. This is often mediated through industry associations and aided by government-financed projects, usually in the form of export subsidies or R&D investments.[75]

(4) For all these reasons, large international companies are much more multinational than they are transnational. They are rooted in *national* economies and *national* systems of production, and they operate through affiliates in other economies. The word "transnational" implies that such international companies are nationally rootless—in effect, organizations unto themselves having neutral, market-rules-dominated relations with all other organizations. This was Richard Barnet and Ronald Müller's argument in the 1970s and, more recently, Robert Reich's. Reich's position is persuasive because he starts from the premise that the world economy has become highly multinationalized and that each nation's wealth depends on its ability to attract international capital as well as to generate international capital, primarily human capital (technological and organizational innovation).[76] For Reich, this translates into a kind of physical-capital neutrality and human-capital nationalness. But he is less convincing when he claims that MNEs, whether Japanese or U.S. or European, do not link the two kinds of capital. Honda does not locate its R&D or corporate control equally in the United States and Japan, and neither does IBM, even though both companies distribute some of these functions to their subsidiaries abroad. Some MNEs come closer to Reich's model than others; and MNEs from any country, when operating in a highly developed country with readily available technical and management skills, are more likely to be "nation neutral" than they would be in a developing country with few such inputs.[77] The very difficulty that MNEs have in delinking physical capital and technological investment from the control of national-origin human capital suggests that MNE nationality counts in regard to how human capital gets employed worldwide.

(5) Yet, there is also a distinct element of anti-Japanese (and anti-Asian) sentiment inherent in U.S. and European Japan-bashing. It is likely that even were the Japanese to lower tariffs and to open up their markets completely to foreign investment, Japanese MNEs would still be successful

---

75. Ibid., p. 30. See also Van Tulder and Junne, *European Multinationals*, chaps. 6 and 7.
76. Reich, *The Work of Nations*. See also Reich's "Who Is Us?"
77. See Gereffi and Newfarmer, "International Oligopoly."

in competing worldwide, owing to their management innovations and technological applications. When Peugeot's President Jacques Calvet says "We must construct Europe for the benefit of Europeans, not the Japanese,"[78] does he also mean that Peugeot cannot compete with Japan, and that Europeans will therefore have to pay higher prices for less reliable automobiles? Which Europeans is Calvet referring to? The real issue is whether Europe and the United States can, indeed, afford to keep the Japanese out, despite their neomercantilist behavior, given their ability to produce technically sophisticated consumer goods and electronic components better than anyone else.

IS THERE STILL A ROLE FOR THE NATION-STATE?

The answer to this question is a resounding yes.

(1) National competitiveness is still a function of national policies, and the attractiveness of economies to foreign multinationals is a function of local economic conditions, including the competitiveness of local labor, the available telecommunications and other infrastructure, and the previous success of the local economy (size of the local market).[79]

One specific *national* policy that has important implications for the attractiveness of an economy as a production site is its investment in human resources, particularly the quality of its educational system. The ability of U.S. automakers to locate sophisticated engine and assembly plants in northern Mexico, for example, is in important part a function of the *trainability* of its local labor, in turn depending on a long-term Mexican policy of rapid educational expansion. The Japanese have insisted that the success of their management system lies in highly schooled Japanese (and, in other locations, non-Japanese) workers who are willing to assume responsibility for quality control.

(2) Local multinationals also depend heavily on national competitive-

---

78. *Fortune*, January 29, 1990, p. 97.

79. See Reich, *Work of Nations*; and Porter, *The Competitive Advantage of Nations*. Porter argues that the "central role of government policy toward the economy is to *deploy a nation's resources (labor and capital) with high and rising levels of productivity.* . . . Government's aim should be to create an environment in which firms can upgrade competitive advantages in established industries [and] . . . to enter new industries where higher productivity can be achieved." (pp. 617–18)

ness, and such competitiveness increasingly depends on human-capital policies, including management training, and on new technology R&D and telecommunications investment: "Knowledge has always been critical in organizing and fostering economic growth. However, the greater the complexity and productivity of an economy, the greater the informational component, and the greater the role played by new knowledge and new applications of knowledge in productivity growth, as compared to the pure addition of production factors such as capital and labor."[80]

Japanese and European governments have made systematic investments as individual nation-states, and the Europeans as part of a regional grouping, in developing new technologies and investing in highly advanced telecommunications infrastructure. The specific purpose of these investments was to make Japanese and European MNEs more competitive in the world economy,[81] a strategy that is particularly effective in "catch-up" technologies, where the technology to be learned is already known.[82] It may be less effective in developing new technologies because the direction of new research is a highly risky venture fraught with dead ends, but such new technologies are increasingly too expensive for most individual firms to handle alone, and this provides yet another reason for national or regional government intervention (see Table 3.3 for European government interventions in electronics from 1968 to 1984).

The payoff to national governments from such investments is that the local economy can become internationally competitive while maintaining national autonomy and—more important—that such investments lead to higher levels of local productivity, providing greater political space for any government. Private companies share this interest because it generates demand for their more sophisticated products, gives them access to highly skilled technicians, workers, and scientists, and allows them to be more competitive on a world scale.

And over the past ten years, the costs of innovation have become so high that it is difficult even for large MNEs to undertake basic research alone. The development of new generations of computer chips, for example, entails astronomical costs. Whereas it is possible to form consortia among companies to develop new technologies, such arrangements appear

80. See Chapter 1, Manuel Castells, "The Informational Economy and the New International Division of Labor."

81. Van Tulder and Junne, European Multinationals, esp. table 6.1.

82. Daniel Okimoto, "Political Context," in Daniel Okimoto, Takuo Sugano, and Franklin B. Weinstein (eds.), Competitive Edge (Stanford: Stanford University Press, 1984).

to be difficult to create and maintain without underlying government finance.

(3) Government policies are also crucial in determining how locally based MNEs are protected from foreign competition. These policies range from direct protection—for example, reserving the local telecommunications or energy markets for domestic, often state-owned, monopolies—to using government procurement programs to stimulate innovation in "national champions," to ideological protection—for example, generating anti-foreign-competition propaganda (in the United States there is a constant stream of government policy statements about Japanese barriers to U.S. investment and exports). On the other hand, a nation-state can pursue a laissez-faire policy regarding foreign investment, leaving domestic capital to fend for itself.

(4) A major issue has to do with what concessions the nation-state gets from domestic or even existing foreign MNEs for these various protections and public investments. Can the government expect private MNEs operating locally to negotiate offshore employment in return for a secure oligopoly position? What degree of cooperation in national R&D consortia should the nation-state expect from MNEs? And, in the case of foreign MNEs, what types of technology transfers to local producers can be gained by government subsidies for basic R&D that are available to all MNEs, regardless of national origin?

Nation-states with larger national markets (or access to regional markets), a highly skilled labor force, well-trained, experienced managers, their own, local MNEs producing similar products, sophisticated infrastructure, and the financial resources to invest heavily in additional infrastructure are obviously in a much better position to get such concessions than those nation-states without such attractive conditions. Unfortunately, Fourth World countries and even newly industrialized countries (NICs) that most need technology transfer through concessions are least likely to get it.

(5) A final word about national human-capital policies. All nation-states have the possibility of developing highly skilled labor forces, but *how* they do so may have a lot to do with their success in a world economy increasingly dominated by information technology. Universities in many countries are not adequately tied into a system of innovation and innovation training. This does not only apply to sciences and engineering, for innovation is just as much an issue in social sciences, business practices, the law, and the arts. Innovative attitudes will also have to extend to

social relations: because of increased migration worldwide, national populations are changing, and subnational movements will demand changes in the concept of the nation-state itself. *The role of the nation-state in creating an innovation society is thus absolutely crucial to the well-being of its citizens in the information age.*

STATE-OWNED MULTINATIONALS

A special way for the nation-state to enter the multinational arena is the state-owned MNE. All such MNEs are located outside the United States and Japan, and many are in the petroleum sector. In 1985, forty-one of the largest two hundred industrial enterprises were state-owned; eighteen of these were multinationals; and seven were French, including Elf-Aquitaine, Renault, CGE, St. Gobain, and Thomson.[83] In 1989, two of the world's ten largest banks were also state-owned: France's Crédit Agricole and Banque Nationale de Paris.

One of the principal purposes of creating such nationalized MNEs is to turn large production units into instruments of national policy—especially when market mechanisms prove to be inefficient. This is often the case in energy, communications, and transportation and in industries that are fundamental to the development of new information technology.

Should such enterprises form an integral part of a progressive agenda in developing domestic MNEs as an alternative to relying on foreign MNEs?

(1) State-owned multinationals already play an important role in Europe, particularly in two crucial sectors: energy and telecommunications. In energy, they are responsible directly to the state to carry out a coordinated energy policy. For all the potential inefficiencies of state enterprises, *overall* European (and state-coordinated Japanese) energy policy has probably been better organized and more effective than the U.S. free-enterprise system.

In communications, the public telecommunications companies have also been able to keep up technologically, as underlined by the fact that in 1985 Thomson got the $4.3 billion order for the new mobile battlefield

83. Jean-Pierre Anastassopoulos, Georges Blanc, and Pierre Dessauge, *State-Owned Multinationals* (New York: John Wiley, 1987), table 1.3.

phone system for the U.S. Army, the largest order ever given by the
Pentagon to a European company.[84] The main problem faced by public
European producers of telecommunications equipment in competing with
the United States or Japan is not that they are owned by the state.
Whether public or private, European firms face much smaller markets in
their principally national base, face different standards of European telecommunications services and a lack of sophistication in European markets.
They are therefore at a disadvantage in exporting into the lucrative U.S.
market. This disadvantage would presumably be at least partially resolved
with standardization of equipment regionally and with competition among
the national companies for regional markets.

On the other hand, in the provision of telecommunications networks,
the public monopolization of services in each nation has retarded business
moves into the widest and most sophisticated uses of computer-telecom-
munications networking. This is true even in France, where the government has pursued an aggressive policy of developing such networks. There
is strong evidence from Japan and the United Kingdom that privatization
of previously public monopolies in telecommunications services has led to
a rapid expansion of networking possibilities, particularly for large firms.[85]

(2) State-owned multinationals theoretically would respond more
quickly to national goals in developing certain technologies, but it is
evident from European-multinational R&D efforts in core technologies
(EUREKA, ESPRIT, BRITE, and RACE) that the dominance of national
champions (in some cases private; in some, public) does not *require* public
ownership for such cooperation. Since even the large and private national
champions are heavily dependent on government subsidies for R&D and
procurement of new technologies (which allow these firms to learn by
doing), they are prepared to enter into consortia deemed useful by their
governments. Thus, public ownership per se is not needed in order to
promote national goals in the policies of today's R&D-dependent, advanced-technology industries.

(3) In addition, there may be considerable contradiction between the
ability of state-owned firms to conform to government political aims and
their ability to be multinationals—that is, to make decisions consistent
with international competitiveness. One analysis argues that those state-

84. Van Tulder and Junne, *European Multinationals*, p. 135.

85. See François Bar and Michael Borrus, "Information Networks and Competitive Advantage:
The Issues for Government Policy and Corporate Strategy" (BRIE, University of California–
Berkeley, October 1989).

owned enterprises which managed to go multinational succeeded in over-coming obstacles imposed by their own governments and developed in host countries strategies comparable with those of private multinationals.[86] At the same time, however, where state-owned firms exist, they often benefit from national foreign policies that promote their expansion: for example, the boost that de Gaulle's aggressive promotion of France in markets dominated by the United States (Canada and Mexico) gave to state-owned French firms, especially Sofretu (underground transport sys-tems). There are many such cases, including the more recent operations of Kuwait's petroleum monopoly and state banks in Europe.

State-owned multinationals make sense, then, when their operations are consistent with a nation-state's foreign policy aims and when their protection at home is not overly costly to the national economy; or when they are crucial to the nation-state's domestic technology policy (i.e., where technology is considered a fundamental infrastructural investment for overall economic development) and that technology policy requires multinational activities. Even so, in the likely situation where a private company can be adequately tied to national goals through government subsidies and procurement policies, state *ownership* may not be necessary.

WHAT ROLE FOR MULTINATIONALS IN THE NATIONAL DEVELOPMENT PROJECT?

Multinational enterprises are powerful economic actors in the interna-tional economy and play a key role in shaping the context in which nation-states formulate their own economic strategies. *But nation-states can also be key actors in shaping what multinationals do.* No case is clearer than the Japanese, in which the nation-state helped create and continues to nourish the tightly woven, export-oriented, R&D-heavy, and govern-ment-protected Japanese multinationals. And although they are latecom-ers, European countries have responded to the relative backwardness of their new information-technological capacity by pursuing aggressive na-tional and regional policies based on R&D consortia. They have also fostered domestic multinationals to serve as "point companies" in building

---

86. Anastassopoulos et al., *State-Owned Multinationals*, p. 103.

a domestic information-technology infrastructure. These policies provide the elements of a national development policy regarding multinationals.

(1) Multinationals should be seen not as friends or foes, but as key components in building a national *capacity to produce*. In this sense, MNEs should be seen as investors in *new forms of national infrastructure*. Such infrastructure is not the traditional roads and railroads, water systems, and power plants, but *information networks and the human skills needed to innovate and manage*.

(2) Information networks are crucial to any domestic industrial policy, and they must be a key element of any progressive political project. Multinationals are dominant precisely in producing many of the products that form these networks. MNEs should be brought into a national information policy in a way that maximizes their contribution to long-run economic growth and social harmony. This means, for some countries (notably LDCs), reducing the foreign-exchange cost of information technology by inducing multinationals to assemble locally those products intended for sale in domestic markets or to form regional markets with a distribution among those countries from MNEs with regional assembly plants. Unfortunately, the more directly promotional local policies are concerning foreign direct investment, the less apparent are the advantages for a nation-state of having the multinational produce locally.

But in the NICs and European countries, including Eastern Europe, more can be demanded by the national development project: foreign MNEs should have to increase steadily the local human-capital component of domestic production and sales. This should include a) local sourcing of increasingly sophisticated components, b) local management, c) local R&D, and d) local autonomy—eventually to the extent that new product strategy and new products for international sale are developed locally.

The concept behind these demands is that the economy's long-run development, including greater equality of income distribution, depends both on the rapid growth of information infrastructure *and* human-resource-intensive jobs. In some sectors, the increasing availability of information technology will increase employment expansion and human-capital intensity. But if manufacturing and some services are to produce increased numbers of higher-level jobs, then R&D capability in those sectors must also increase. The national development project should be identified as developing a policy that makes MNEs most responsible to national welfare and most willing to compromise—to transfer managerial training and technological skills to locals, and to keep domestic MNEs most rooted in domestic policy. It should always be remembered that the advantage of having MNEs depends on the continued attractiveness of whatever got them there in the first place and on the extent to which they transfer firm-specific assets—particularly organizational capability, the capacity to innovate, and knowledge about manufacturing processes and product delivery (marketing, finance, sales).

(3) One way to keep foreign MNEs in oligopolized sectors "honest" and to root domestic MNEs in domestic policy is to develop local R&D consortia and national champions, as the Europeans and Japanese have already done. This is particularly effective in telecommunications and will become even more effective in computers as "open architecture" and plug-in systems become the norm. Smaller national producers are already able to sell to IBM users because of such changes.

State-owned multinationals also make sense in some sectors, especially petroleum and energy more generally. In other sectors, however, state-owned multinationals may not work nearly so well as *state-tied* MNEs, and the progressive political project should avoid committing itself to state ownership.

(4) What about the Japanese? Are they unfair competitors? Should national or even regional development projects try, officially or unofficially, to hinder the spread of Japanese multinationals?

Again, the real issue should be whether the entry of a particular Japanese multinational improves the nation's economic and social development. What does the MNE bring in, and what is the likelihood that it will transfer information and human-capital infrastructure? How does its contribution compare with that of local firms producing the same product? In the case of Japanese automobile manufacturers, for example, what is the trade-off between their higher-quality, lower-price product and the lesser likelihood (compared to domestic firms) that they will site R&D and strategic management decisions in the host country? In the United States, for example, U.S. manufacturers are steadily moving their production to Mexico; in their desire to appear "American," will the "new" Japanese producers actually locate a higher percentage of their U.S. production in the United States and export fewer jobs?

In many countries, including the United States, but especially in Europe, the entry of Japanese multinationals could very well force local MNEs to become more competitive in domestic and regional markets. Joint ventures between local and Japanese firms are another possibility already taking place.

The old formulas for protecting inefficient local industries are probably anachronistic, and it is also anachronistic to believe that local firms will be able to provide the wide range of information technology and managerial skills needed to move into the twenty-first century. On the other hand, local human-capital development and the R&D financing to go with it are also crucial to national and regional progress. MNEs must be judged by their willingness to train people everywhere for participation in the world's information economy. If they are unwilling to train locals for jobs that require new knowledge and new skills—skills that would then become part of the local human-capital stock employable in local firms—their contribution to long-run local development will be small. Other forms of bringing new technology into the local economy might be much more productive in increasing economic development and creating new knowledge. The Japanese, after all, never relied on foreign investment in their technological development, only on learning from experts brought to Japan to teach the Japanese new methods directly. Yet, if multinationals are willing to train and educate and transfer knowledge as part of the "deal," whereby they will gain access to local markets or other local resources, then the location of an MNC in a particular country could be a rapid and efficient way of stimulating new types of production and facilitating the acquisition of new methods locally. In today's rapidly changing world economy, this may also be one of the few ways that nation-states can get access to such learning.

Stephen S. Cohen

4

Geo-Economics: Lessons from America's Mistakes

Fundamental changes in the world economy are rapidly reordering the hierarchy of wealth and power among nations. That the U.S. economy is navigating that transition badly should by now be evident, although the implications of the difficulties for Europe as well as for the United States are uncertain and discomforting. At the moment, however, the very real problems of the European economies are concealed by the dynamism and enthusiasm generated by an acceleration of European integration and by the opening of a new European frontier to the East.

In this chapter, I would like to depart from the newly dominant tone of Europhoria and concentrate on a particular set of difficult economic and societal questions that will not prove amenable to traditional solutions. For Europe has a choice. It can respond creatively to the challenges of this transition, enhance its wealth and power, and in the process find itself structuring a better society; or it can, as the United States has, set out in the wrong direction, erode its power and wealth, and create a less prosperous, less generous, less just, and less secure society. Such a fatal choice begins with denial, with a failure (or refusal) to recognize the new nature of economic challenges. Denial is an easily attained attitude: it is supported by the mass of established interests and practices, by the momentum of prosperity, by the force of greater, more dramatic issues, and by the authority of conventional economics. But in this moment Europe can ill afford denial. Although the economic choices facing Europe are not played out at the level of high politics, they are nonetheless crucial and will affect the Community profoundly. Europe might learn how to better make these choices by considering the American economic experience of the last decade.

THE NATURE OF THE TRANSITION

Two distinct sets of fundamental forces are driving the transition in the international economy. The first set consists of basic changes in both the extent and the nature of international competition. The second set— cumulating innovations in the organization of production—is displacing mass production as the dominant mode of production with something new that we can call high-volume flexible production. American producers have experienced the impact of these changes more extensively and more suddenly than their European counterparts in sectors ranging from semiconductors and lasers to computers and controllers, from automobiles, outboard motors, and lawn mowers to clothing, retailing, and insurance.

The New Extent of International Competition

As recently as the late 1960s, foreign competition was a marginal phenomenon in the U.S. economy. Despite the success of successive rounds of GATT (General Agreement on Tariffs and Trade), and a commitment to an increasingly open economy, trade numbers remained small; imports (or exports) rarely exceeded 4 percent of GNP. More significantly, their composition did not threaten many major sectors. Indeed, the biggest trade flow was with Canada, and trade was conducted in such a way as to deny the basic notion and force of foreign competition: the most important loop was in automobiles, and it was confined to interplant transfers within the big-three American companies. Today, however, about 70 percent of everything we make is subject to direct, or imminent, competition from foreign-based companies. Competition now strikes at the fundamental competence and even the existence of major American industries and companies. This change is so huge and so sudden that it qualifies as revolutionary.

Europe's experience here is quite different. For Europeans, international competition is not new, and the movement toward the Single Market has vastly intensified that competition. But it is still overwhelmingly intra-European. Conventional statistics show Europe accounting for some 43 percent of world imports; however, if one combines the twelve European Community nations with the EFTA (European Free-Trade Association) to eliminate intra-European trade from the data, Europe's share of world imports suddenly shrinks to 12 percent.[1] On a per capita basis, Europe imports only one-fourth as much manufactured goods from Asia as America.[2] With the important exception of a large set of U.S.-based multinational companies, for the most part long established in Europe, competition from foreign-based suppliers (transplants) is only just beginning to be a serious fact of European life.

The small volume of extra-European industrial imports and the still small force that extra-European competition exerts on the European economy leave Europe's exposure to international competition—in the sense of a major force reshaping European life—still intermediary between the United States' exposure in the early 1970s and the United States' exposure now. Despite all likely efforts to maintain this situation, it will not persist for long.

The New Nature of International Competition

International competition has changed as much in its nature as in its extent. The important change is not, as is so commonly held, a geographic shift from the Atlantic to the Pacific. Rather, it concerns the rise of the "developmental state" and its impact upon the world trade and development system.[3] The developmental state defines a new set of arrangements between the state, society, and industry designed to change the structure

1. Gerard Lafay and Colette Herzog with Loukas Stemitsiotis and Deniz Unal, *Commerce International: La Fin des Avantages Acquis* (Paris: *Economica*, for Centre d'Etudes Prospectives et d'Informations Internationales, 1989), pp. 55–57.

2. Ibid., p. 53.

3. The Developmental State is Chalmers Johnson's phrase. See his important *MITI and the Japanese Miracle* (Stanford: Stanford University Press, 1982).

of the nation's comparative advantage. Such arrangements, of course, were first and most effectively developed in Japan but are now being imitated, with varying degrees of success, in several countries. Japan pioneered a set of institutional innovations. These include 1) the state as a Gatekeeper, determining what can enter the Japanese economy (and under what conditions), including technology and direct investment as well as product; 2) a *keiretsu* system, which reinforces the state's gatekeeper role and creates loose "virtual integration" on a massive new scale; and 3) the capability to target key technologies and promote domestic industry by channeling cheap capital, promoting lively (but controlled) competition among Japanese companies, and encouraging early forays into outside markets to hone competitiveness.

The result is not simply that Japan enjoys a surplus in its balance of payments or that the United States runs deficits. That is largely—but not entirely—a macroeconomic matter. The important result of this fundamental change in the system is strategic. It is to be found in the composition of trade and the resulting rate and structure of industrial development. Its significance lies in the cumulative creation, over time, of a new and superior structure of comparative (and competitive) advantage in Japan and a corresponding weakening of those capabilities in its trading partners. It also has a destabilizing system effect on the world trade and development system.

The postwar international trade regime was based upon two fundamental ideas: trade would be intrasectoral, and direct foreign investment through multinational corporations (MNCs) would be a major vehicle of market penetration. Both would operate on a large scale without devastating the industrial and social landscapes of trading partners. As Figures 4.1–4.4 indicate, Japan is an exception to the fundamental pattern of trade on which the postwar international economic order was predicated: that is, intrasectoral specialization.

For both France and Germany, for example, automobiles are the leading export, accounting for more than 11 percent of total manufactured exports for France and about 16 percent for Germany. The important point, however, is that automobiles are also one of the highest-volume import sectors in both France and Germany. The Figures demonstrate a pattern of substantial imports in those same sectors where the nation is a strong exporter. For France, five of the top-ten import categories are among the top-ten export categories. The Japanese pattern is fundamentally and distinctively different. Crudely put, Japan does not import in those sectors

Figure 4.1. Manufactured exports and imports for France as percent of total exports, 1991.

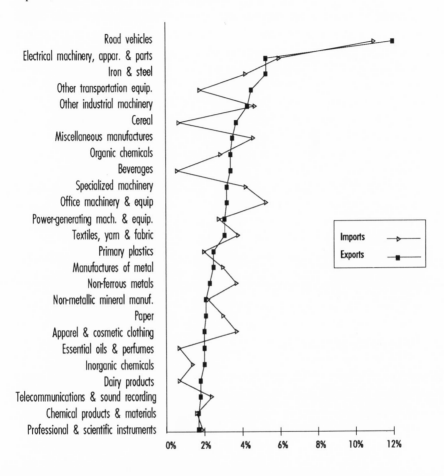

SOURCE: OECD, *Foreign Trade by Commodities* (Paris, 1992).

where it is a major exporter. There are many possible explanations for this distinctive and system-destabilizing pattern. They are not our immediate concern here; the effects, however, are. It has been intrasectoral trade that has permitted international trade to grow—often faster than GNP in the postwar period—in ways that have been largely beneficial to all parties without creating a predatory pattern of large-scale, sectoral devastation among trading partners. Absent such a pattern of intrasectoral

Figure 4.2. Manufactured exports and imports for Germany as percent of total exports, 1990.

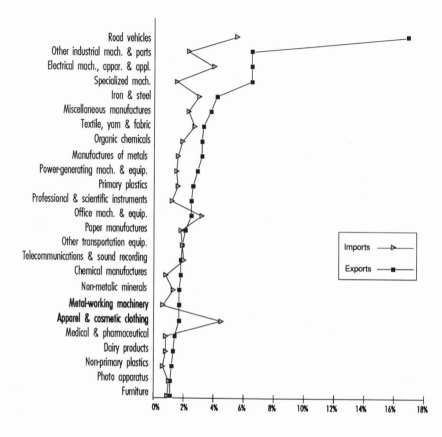

Source: OECD, *Foreign Trade by Commodities* (Paris, 1991).

trade, international trade becomes a process of one nation wiping out large sectors (e.g., autos) in another. Trade becomes fundamentally predatory and unstable.

The multinational corporation, not simple imports and exports, was the postwar device for transatlantic economic penetration and technology transfer without economic devastation. The Japanese state, acting as gatekeeper, was able to break up the package of product, technology, capital, and control that is the MNC, and to reassemble those pieces in

Figure 4.3. Manufactured exports and imports for the United States as percent of total exports, 1990.

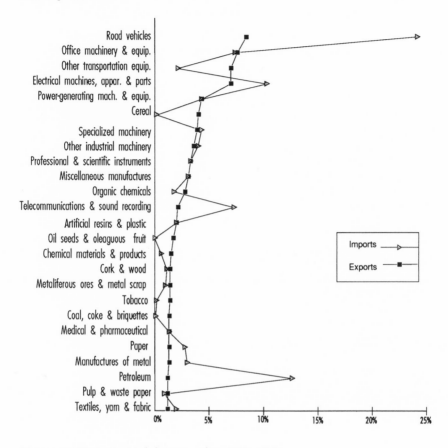

SOURCE: OECD, *Foreign Trade by Commodities* (Paris, 1992).

Japan, under Japanese control. With a handful of conspicuous exceptions, neither U.S. nor European MNCs were able to leverage their early lead in technology, quality, and volume into sustainable major-market positions in Japan. Advantages in product innovation could quickly be nullified in the Japanese market, where economies of scale and scope would accumulate, and the outcome would be decided as a manufacturing game. This story was repeated in sector after sector—in automobiles, consumer electronics, and semiconductors. Now Japan is changing. The capital

Figure 4.4.   Manufactured exports and imports for Japan as percent of total exports, 1989.

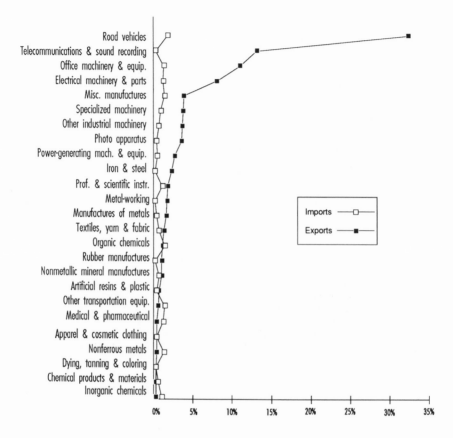

SOURCE: OECD, *Foreign Trade by Commodities* (Paris, 1990).

market is much more open today than it was just a few years ago, and with real consequences. But despite rapid change, the fundamental pattern is still very much in place, especially in newly targeted industries.

Figure 4.5 records a fundamental asymmetry in direct foreign investment. With only a few conspicuous exceptions, American and European multinationals have not been able to establish themselves in Japan. Foreign companies still represent less than 1 percent of all Japanese industrial output, while they account for more than ten times that much in the

Figure 4.5. Foreign ownership as percent of industrial output in selected countries, 1988.

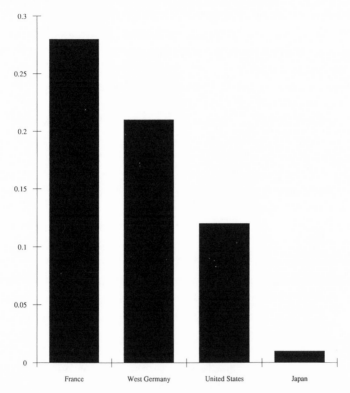

SOURCE: France, Commissariat Général du Plan, *Rapport sur les invetissements internationaux* (April 1992).

United States, and more than twenty times that in the larger European countries.

Thus, the twin equilibriating mechanisms of the international system—intrasectoral trade and direct industrial investment—have been unable to function in Japan. Despite the failure, or refusal, of the U.S. government (as well as most American economists) to recognize it, government policy plays a critical role in determining outcomes in the new international economic order, more so now than ever. And not just in sui generis Japan.

A Revolution in the Organization of Production

The second set of epochal changes driving the transition in the international economy is of a different nature. It is defined by a fundamental change in complex manufacturing, a change of revolutionary import in the process of production. Though largely a Japanese innovation, this revolutionary change is in no way bound by national policy, ethnicity, or culture. Like the mass-production revolution which preceded it on the trajectory of cutting-edge industrial development and which had its origins in the United States, this new approach, which we can call high-volume flexible production, or velocity production, or "lean" production, can be learned by Americans and Europeans. The problem is that despite many important exceptions, they have not yet learned it. And they must. For flexible-volume production commands a decisive competitive advantage over traditional mass production, and it strikes at the heart of the wealth-generating activities of the advanced nations: the manufacture of automobiles, trucks, washing machines, televisions, and the rest—a truly vast array of products.

Why is flexible-volume production of such importance and not just another easily adapted innovation? Because it is not a quickly learned gimmick, nor is it embodied in machinery that can be purchased, nor can its cumulating advantages over traditional mass production be overcome by intensified investment in mass production combined with cheaper labor. It must be learned and developed through far-reaching and painful organizational change. And it commands in its realm a truly decisive advantage over traditional mass production, even when well done, as by the best European auto producers. In the case of automobiles, lean production uses less of everything compared with mass production: half the number of human work hours in the factory, half the manufacturing space, half the investment in tools and machinery, half the engineering hours to develop a new product, and half the time to develop that product. It also requires less than half the needed inventory on site, turns out products with far fewer defects, and yields a greater and growing variety of products.[4] It represents, in brief, almost as decisive an advantage over mass production as mass production represented over craft production.

4. James P. Womack et al., *The Machine That Changed the World* (New York, 1990), p. 13. The following description of high-volume flexible production (or, as Womack et al. call it, "lean production") draws heavily on that truly excellent and accessible study. I have found it to be the clearest and best documented presentation of the revolution in production, and am greatly indebted to the Womack team. I hope that more researchers—and policymakers—will quickly acquire an indebtedness to their work. For a more intellectually rich and nuanced description, see the excellent analysis on Japanese production by Benjamin Coriat, *Penser à l'Envers* (Paris, 1991). See also Fugimoto and Clark.

The consequences for the competitive positions of nations, and for the organization of society, may be similarly potent.

Table 4.1 summarizes a complex story, comparing the performance of Japanese, U.S., and European auto-assembly plants. It is worth studying carefully. Japan's position relative to the United States is striking: one-third fewer labor hours per car, one-tenth the inventory carried, and nearly one-third fewer defects. These differences are at the heart of the compounding crisis the American automobile industry faces, a crisis that is growing worse despite protectionist quotas and despite what is now several years of rapid and significant improvements prompted by a hugely

Table 4.1.   Auto-Assembly Plant Characteristics, 1989 (Plant Averages by Global Region)

	Japanese in Japan	Japanese in N. America	American in N. America	All Europe
Performance				
Productivity (hrs./vehicle)	16.8	21.2	25.1	36.2
Quality (assembly defects/100 vehicles)	60.0	65.0	82.3	97.0
Layout				
Space (sq. ft./vehicle/yr.)	5.7	9.1	7.8	7.8
Size of repair area (% of assembly space)	4.1	4.9	12.9	14.4
Inventories (days for 8 sample parts)	.2	1.6	2.9	2.0
Work force				
Percent of work force in teams	69.3	71.3	17.3	.6
Job rotation (0 = none, 4 = frequent)	3.0	2.7	.9	1.9
Suggestions/employee	61.6	1.4	.4	.4
Number of job classes	11.9	8.7	67.1	14.8
Training of new production workers (hrs.)	380.3	370.0	46.4	173.3
Absenteeism (days/employee)	5.0	4.8	11.7	12.1
Automation				
Welding (% of direct steps)	86.2	85.0	76.2	76.6
Painting (% of direct steps)	54.6	40.7	33.6	38.2
Assembly (% of direct steps)	1.7	1.1	1.2	3.1

SOURCE: IMVP world assembly plant survey, 1989; J. D. Power initial quality survey, 1989.

painful and costly bloodletting. Indeed, quite a few American plants are now beginning to reach recent Japanese norms, although too many more still have a long way to go.

What should be most striking is that the European plants are well behind the American plants in regard to performance. Variable by critical variable, the story is the same. European automobiles are fundamentally—not marginally—more costly to make than Japanese cars, and they are not as well made. They take twice as much direct labor, half again as much plant space, ten times as much costly inventory waiting around, and, at the end, they have half again as many defects. (This applies to the European mass-production firms: Volkswagen, Renault, Peugeot, FIAT, etc. The custom mass producers such as Mercedes and BMW are, despite ardent wishes to the contrary, no better situated and no better protected; the recent drubbing they have taken from Toyota in the U.S. market should, finally, alert them to their problems.)

Let me again stress that this huge and disquieting difference in performance is not the result of more massive accumulations of capital in the production of Japanese cars, nor the result of newer machinery, cheaper labor, nor even tighter discipline. It is not a phenomenon of national culture. It is certainly not lodged in the culture of the work force (management may be another question). Witness the superior performance of those Japanese transplants in the United States which use American labor. The overwhelming difference in performance stems directly from a fundamentally different approach to the organization of production: that is, to the organization of the firm and the production process. Similar differences can be found in other industrial applications of complex manufacturing. More and cheaper capital, less and cheaper labor will not restore European competitiveness. We are dealing with a new mode of production. What is called for is a fundamental reorganization of the production process extending up through corporate management and not just confined to the shop floor. And that is neither easy nor quick nor amenable to executive decree.

High-Volume Flexible Production

Craft production came first. It was Europe's great strength. The craft producer uses highly skilled workers and simple but flexible tools. Products are customized to demand. Each unit is expensive. Claims are often made for high quality, which usually resides in hard-to-measure attributes. But aside from special, luxury ingredients (equally available to velocity producers) and hang-on features (also equally available), those claims, as in the case of "crafted" mass-production European luxury cars, are overinflated.[5]

Mass production began in the United States in the early nineteenth century with the production of interchangeable parts for guns in response to shortages of skilled gunsmiths. Almost a century later, Henry Ford put all the pieces together: interchangeable parts; a minute division of the work process; complex, expensive, and specialized machinery; a moving assembly line; highly trained and highly specialized people to design the product and to design, organize, and run the production process; and large numbers of unskilled (or low-skilled) people to perform the simplest, most minutely choreographed tasks of making the product.

"Fordism," as European sociologists are fond of calling this system, conquered the industrial heartland once occupied by craft production. Its economic advantages were simply stupendous: almost 90 percent less direct labor per vehicle when compared with the most advanced form of craft production (which used interchangeable parts) and, unlike craft production, a potential for steady improvement through automation.[6] Fordism became the model of how to produce in an advanced economy and (after World War II) came to dominate European production—but not before creating a huge disparity in wealth and power between the United States and Europe. Mass production meant high-volume production of standardized products for what was an unusually homogeneous as well as vast market; and it made that market even more homogeneous. The result was high productivity and high wages for both unskilled and skilled labor, and cheap, quality products—formerly obtainable only by the rich—to buy with those high wages. Around the mass production system a vast array of social structures came into being, from the industrial union to defend workers' interests to the business school to teach "management," that is, the systematic coordination and measurement of complex activities at a hitherto unknown scale. Mass production gave our institutions and even our societies their present form; that is the main reason it is proving so difficult to change in fundamental ways and on a vast scale.

Simply put, mass production was the greatest production system in the

---

5. For convincing evidence, drive a Lexus.

6. Womack et al., op. cit., fig. 2.1. Again, this description of "lean production" follows Womack. For an earlier and cruder description, see Cohen and Zysman, *Manufacturing Matters*, 1987; see also Abegglen and Stalk, *Kaisha* (1985), and Imai, *Kaizen* (1986).

history of the world. It won the war; and by dissolving social conflicts in a rising tide of consumer goods, it won the peace. It catapulted America into a unique position of overweening economic, military, political, and cultural power. It had, however, its weaknesses. It was terribly inflexible. Products could not be changed easily. Truly massive accumulations of capital, massive bureaucratic planning, and, especially, very long production runs were its well-known secrets. And the runs were long. In the heyday of the system, 1955, some 7 million cars were made in the United States. Despite a plethora of styles, some 80 percent of those cars were variants of just six models.[7] That was also the year when the U.S. auto industry produced almost three-quarters of all the world's automobiles. Then their market share began to decline steadily—but for good, not bad, reasons. By the late 1950s recovery was long completed in Europe and mass production was taking hold. The European auto industry (as well as a broad suit of other industries) set out to copy the American mass-production model and began to achieve their goals at Wolfsburg, Flins, and Mirafiori. They even began to imitate Detroit (though thirty years later) by importing cheap and supposedly docile foreign labor to take the assembly-line jobs.

The real drama was elsewhere, in Japan, but it remained long concealed from American and European attention. One might just as well call volume-flexible production or lean production the "Toyota system" or "Toyotaism."

In 1962 Detroit produced more cars in a week than Japan produced in a year. During the 1950s or sixties or even the seventies, Toyota had no possibility of successfully competing with Ford, or with FIAT, Volkswagen, Renault, or Austin. But they didn't have to. The Japanese government succeeded in keeping the Americans and the Europeans out of the Japanese auto market. Foreigners could not import product; nor could they establish subsidiaries to produce in Japan. They could only license technology, which eventually the weakest of them did. Without these thirty years of complete protection, Japan's story would be very different. Whatever neoclassical economists may argue, this is clearly a case where protectionism worked. And it is not a trivial case.

The rest of the story, however, is a tale of inspired Japanese innovation. Eiji Toyoda and his brilliant chief engineer, Taiichi Ohno, are generally credited with masterminding the series of organizational innovations that

7. Ibid., p. 43.

cumulated in the volume-flexible production system and the Japanese triumph in automobiles which lies behind the meteoric rise of Japanese economic, financial, and technological power. Aided, it turned out, by powerful constraints—very little capital and a small market—Toyota improvised fundamental innovations. Instead of dedicating huge die presses to making a specific part (standard practice in Detroit) Toyota worked out ways to change dies quickly, ultimately in a matter of minutes, thus permitting much shorter runs and radically economizing on capital and inventory. An astonishing discovery was made: when all indirect costs were added up, it actually cost less per part to make small batches this way, by quick die changes, than to organize for dedicated equipment and enormous runs. But implementing this approach meant passing the responsibility for changing dies to the line workers, not to specialized teams as in the mass-production plants of the West.

This led to a second innovation that gave authority to stop the line to the line workers, something unheard of (to this day) in most Western plants. If something was wrong in a Detroit plant, it was put aside for rework; the line kept moving (and defects kept piling up for rework). Eventually, but not always, teams of specialists descended to analyze the problem and to plan changes. At Toyota, the line would stop at the first sign of a defect; the work team would undertake a simple but extensive diagnostic drill until they could find the cause of the problem and fix it. Eventually the Toyota line, which could be stopped by any worker, stopped less frequently than the American or European lines which are never supposed to stop.

The reward here was the end of the classic trade-off: quality for price. Toyota achieved higher quality (no defects) at lower price. A Toyota plant now has almost no area at the end of the assembly line for rework. An American or European plant uses some 20 percent of the floor space for this function which eats up about 25 percent of labor time! According to Womack, those skilled craftsmen in white lab coats at the end of the Mercedes line, so prominently featured in the advertisements, are skillfully fixing defects. They shouldn't be there in the first place. Their work represents waste. And this rework phase amounts to over 25 percent of the direct labor (and probably more of the indirect labor).[8] Jaguar is even worse—a primitive mess: Their greatest investments in recent years have been in customer service—again, fixing defects in gay profusion. By

8. Ibid., pp. 88–91.

comparison with Renault or Mercedes, the Toyota line yields almost no defects. There is no rework area. There are no skilled craftsmen either doing rework at the end of the line or posing for advertising photos.

The emblematics of this revolutionary new production system are becoming well known: "just-in-time" production; total quality; zero defects; rapid cycle time; design for manufacturability. Other companies are now experimenting with these production innovations. Again, on average, the Americans are way ahead of the Europeans. What they discover, if they do it right, is that each of these innovations is a different door into the same system: a completely new organization of the firm and its relations with supplier firms that dramatically shrinks the hierarchy (many fewer white-collar jobs) and radically redistributes power within the enterprise downward, to the shop floor. It puts a premium on formal skills in the work force, radically reduces the number of outside suppliers and establishes a new kind of working relationship between final assembler and supplier, and it often provokes significant locational perturbations as suppliers try to bunch up close to final users. Mostly it means radical changes in human relations and organizational structures in and around the companies. This is the hardest part.

High-volume flexible production is a decisively superior approach to production in a broad set of industries: the very industries that constitute the heartland of the European economy. It is not "buyable," in the sense of being lodged in tools and equipment. It is not easy to set up; a few executive orders cannot close the gap. But there is no way to stay competitive over time without changing to high-volume flexible production. For the large organizations that dominate the European economy, the change will be, at best, painful and will generate serious dislocations and problems. The fact that the Japanese auto producers out-produced American giants is well known, although its modalities deserve more careful attention than they have received. Table 4.1 shows that the European producers are in even worse shape than the American producers and, whatever they may think, they have not yet felt the direct, bloodletting shock of massive direct competition to force them to improve while, at the same time, depriving them of the means and the time to make those improvements.

AMERICA'S RESPONSE TO THE TRANSITION

How has the U.S. economy responded to the basic transition in the international economy, driven by radical changes in the extent of international competition, in the nature of international competition (the rise of the developmental state), and in the organization of production?

There is no single indicator of the competitive performance of a giant national economy, no proverbial "bottom line." However, a large number of individual indicators—like the pixels on the flat panel display that U.S. and European companies both seem to have such difficulty producing— produce a picture. The picture is not encouraging.

The most dramatic indicator of a troubled U.S. adjustment to the new dynamics of international competition is America's gargantuan trade deficit. Figure 4.6 charts its growth. A trade deficit, however, or even a deficit in current accounts is not by itself necessarily bad. The United States ran a trade deficit for well over the first hundred years of its existence, borrowing money in Europe to purchase the capital goods that permitted its rapid industrialization. But for almost a hundred years, until the early 1970s, the U.S. ran a surplus in its merchandise trade. Since the early 1970s it has run a deficit, and that deficit has grown to a hitherto unimaginable and currently unmanageable scale.

The current U.S. deficit differs from deficits of early U.S. history in two important ways. First, it is not the result of imported investment goods that in the long term will improve the fundamental productivity of

Figure 4.6. U.S. merchandise trade deficit, annualized, 1966–1990.

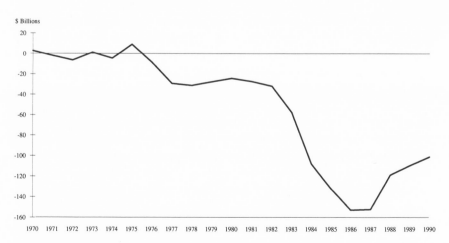

SOURCE: Berkeley Roundtable on the International Economy.

the U.S. economy and thereby provide the means for an improved U.S. trade balance and a re-equilibrium at the world level. Second, its colossal scale threatens the stability of the world economy whether it continues at its present rate or even if the trade flow should somehow suddenly and massively reverse and the U.S. balance turn positive.

America cannot continue to run such a trade deficit indefinitely. From the viewpoint of European exporters, this is a discouraging prospect. Indeed, unless there is a marked increase in the rate of economic growth in the world, especially in the nations we once called the Third World, it is hard to imagine Europe and Japan adjusting to a $100-billion-per-year reversal in American trade flow. The first problem is simple to state, though difficult to answer: Who would buy the products of an American export boom on the scale needed to bring the deficit down to zero? The problem becomes truly horrendous if we add to that reversal a U.S. trade surplus sufficient to reduce America's net foreign indebtedness.

Figure 4.7 shows America's concomitant fall into deep debt. It traces an unprecedented descent from the world's largest creditor (up through the early 1980s) to the world's largest debtor by 1987. That debt should now

Figure 4.7. Net U.S. international investment position, 1971–1987.

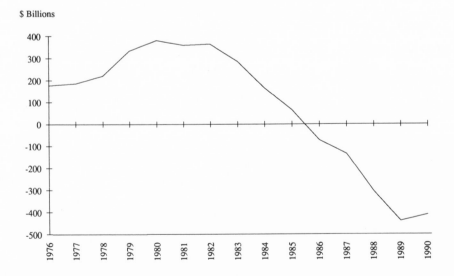

$ Billions

SOURCE: U.S. Department of Commerce, Bureau of Economic Analysis, *Survey of Current Business* (Washington, D.C.: GPO, June 1987), table 1.

extend well past $600 billion. It will be managed by engaging, on a massive scale, in "debt-equity" swaps, a vocabulary and technique developed by U.S. bankers for Latin America's basket-case debts. But the real debt-for-equity swap will not be between the United States and Latin America; it will be between Japan and the United States. As the United States has a sufficient quantity of salable economic assets to sustain a sell-off for several presidential administrations, shortage may manifest itself in America's stock of political capital long before an absolute depletion of America's economic capital. The debt, however, can neither be written off nor paid off; it can only be "serviced" at steadily increasing amounts, imposing a growing negative effect on the U.S. commercial balance and an increasingly depressive effect on U.S. living standards. At present, the U.S. government is organizing a major "crash" program to revise American economic statistics in order to eliminate—in the official statistics—America's accumulated debtor position. By the 1992 presidential elections, a new series should show America out of the red. Yet, unless a genuine reversal occurs, the U.S. debt will continue to grow. It is just one of many time bombs ticking away beneath the international economy.

The size of the trade deficit is a macroeconomic phenomenon, and so is the debt. According to conventional economic theory, the deficit does not say much about U.S. competitiveness. A less conventional view would argue that it has enormous implications for economies of scale and scope, for the cost of capital, for the ability to invest, etc. and therefore does directly impact competitiveness. Whatever meaning one reads into the scale of the deficit, its composition says much about the competitive position of the U.S. economy.

Official report after official report documents the major declines of U.S. market share in critical sectors of advanced technology (except for aerospace).[9] Figure 4.8 analyzes America's trade deficit with our major trading partners. If we set aside Canada and the OPEC nations as special situations what stands out is that the United States has no serious trade imbalance with Europe, but does have a vast and seemingly intractable deficit with Japan and the NICs (newly industrialized countries).

Productivity is the economist's favorite proxy for national economic performance. Ultimately, it is what makes for higher incomes and greater competitiveness. As Figure 4.9 indicates, U.S. productivity is still the

9. See, for example, *Handbook of Economic Statistics*, Central Intelligence Agency, 1989, fig. 15, p. 18. See also the *Competitive Status of the U.S. Electronics Sector*, U.S. Department of Commerce, 1990.

Figure 4.8. U.S. trade deficit with major trading partners, 1989.

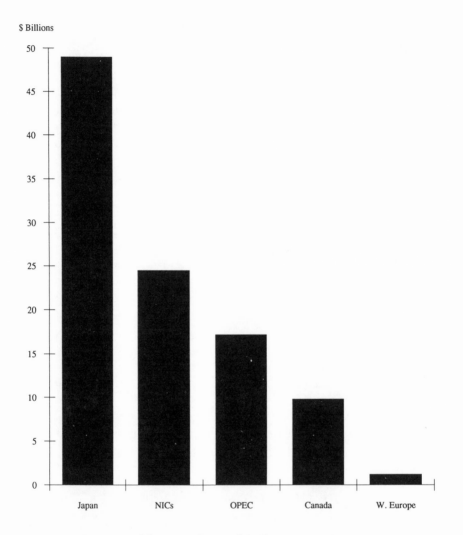

$ Billions

SOURCE: U.S. Department of Commerce, Bureau of the Census.

NOTE: NICs = newly industrialized countries (South Korea, Taiwan, Singapore, and Hong Kong); OPEC = Organization of Petroleum-Exporting Countries.

Figure 4.9. Relative levels of real GDP per employed person in selected countries, 1960–1990.

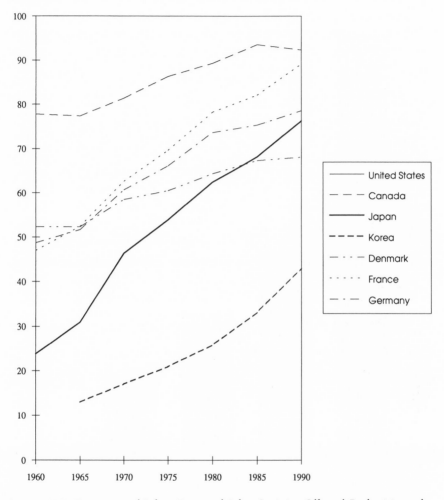

SOURCE: U.S. Department of Labor, Bureau of Labor Statistics, Office of Productivity and Technology, January 1992.

highest; but Table 4.2 tells a more interesting story, and is less vulnerable to the dangers of comparing GNP levels. Across a full generation, from 1960–90, U.S. productivity growth lagged well behind all of the other G-7 nations. In brief, it charts the squandering of America's enormous economic lead.

R&D (Figure 4.10) and investment rates (Figure 4.11) are major determinants of productivity. U.S. investment has been lagging and continues to lag behind its closest competitors. In 1991, Japan invested about two times as much per capita as the U.S.

Keynes taught that savings rates (Figure 4.12) do not determine investment rates; they merely limit them. In an open world economy they should not very significantly affect the availability or the cost of capital.

Table 4.2.   Annual Percent Changes in Manufacturing Productivity, G-7 Nations, 1960–1990

	United States	Canada	Japan	France	Germany	Italy	United Kingdom
1960–90	2.9	2.9	6.9	4.9	4.0	5.3	3.7
1960–73	3.3	4.5	10.2	6.4	5.6	6.4	4.2
1973–79	2.5	2.1	5.0	4.6	4.2	5.7	1.2
1979–90	3.1	1.5	4.1	3.2	2.1	3.9	4.4

SOURCE: Arthur Neef and Christopher Kask, "Manufacturing Productivity and Labor Costs in 14 Economies," *Monthly Labor Review* (December 1991), table 2.

NOTE: Rates of change based on the compound-rate method.

Figure 4.10.   Investment: nondefense R&D expenditure.

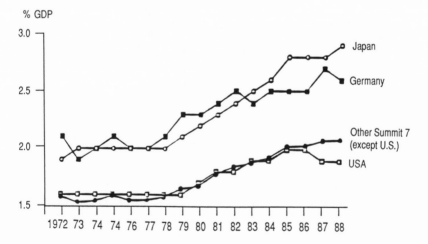

SOURCE: Council on Competitiveness and OECD National Accounts.

Figure 4.11. Investment: private industry expenditure on plant and equipment.

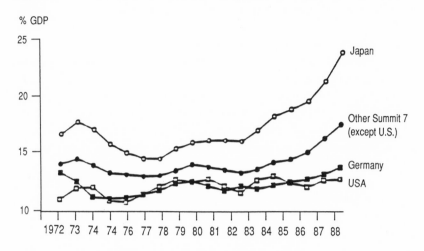

SOURCE: Council on Competitiveness and OECD National Accounts.

Figure 4.12. Gross savings as percent of GNP: 1947–1990 (national saving was below its historical average in the 1980s).

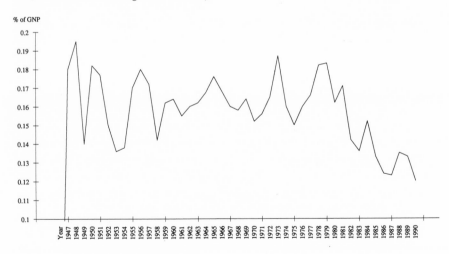

SOURCE: U.S. Department of Commerce.

But they do. Note the drop in the U.S. savings rate for the period after 1980, when the Reagan administration launched its policies intended to favor private savings. These included cuts in spending on social programs and on public infrastructure, high real interest rates, and a radical reduction of upper bracket income taxes to redistribute income toward the top.

Real wages in the United States (Figure 4.13) have not increased at all since the early 1970s. Indeed, they are now no higher than they were in the early 1960s; and they fell, in absolute terms, during the 1980s. With a few brief and painful exceptions, this is the first time in some two hundred years that this has happened in the United States. The American constitutional bargain is predicated on an assumption of permanently rising real wages. That compact has not been honored, and the future does not promise a major reversal any time soon. The comparison with Europe and Japan is striking. For it was not high and growing wage costs that eroded America's international trade position; as America's trade position deteriorated, wage differentials narrowed and then vanished. The stagnation of American real wages may have had a more telling effect on saving rates than the increase in income share going to the rich—and almost all the increase went to the rich, not to the so-called middle class.

Figure 4.14 charts the cumulative effect of steadily increasing income inequality. It covers the period from 1977 to the present. Dividing Americans by income, into quintiles, it shows that the bottom fifth suffered an absolute loss of 12 percent in their after-tax income over that fifteen-year period. The next quintile lost 10 percent of their income, and the third quintile, the "middle of the middle," saw their real income decline by 8 percent after fifteen years of effort and weak national growth. The fourth quintile broke even: Their income rose by a token 1 percent over fifteen years. Only the top fifth benefited from the American social contract—and even they did so quite unequally among themselves. Those in the top eightieth to ninetieth percentiles saw their after-tax income rise by 8 percent—that is, less than half of a percent per year. Those falling between the ninetieth to ninety-fifth percentiles scored about the same, a weak 9 percent. The top 5 percent, however, did much better. Those above the ninety-fifth percentile—but below the magic top 1 percent—saw their incomes grow by a meager 23 percent over fifteen years, under 1.5 percent per year while watching the top 1% boost their income by 136 percent. In the America of the 1980s, income was redistributed toward the top, perhaps more literally than most Americans imagined. Not many realized how few would be in that favored group.

Figure 4.13.   U.S. average weekly real earnings in private nonagricultural industry, 1950–1991.

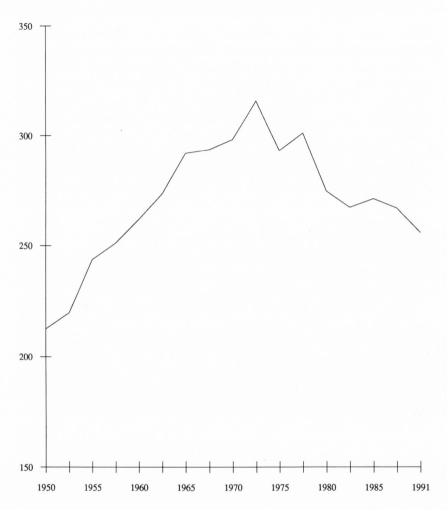

SOURCE: U.S. Department of Labor, Bureau of Labor Statistics Labstat Series Report.

INDEX: 1982 = 100.

Figure 4.14.   Percent change in U.S. personal income after taxes, 1977–1992.

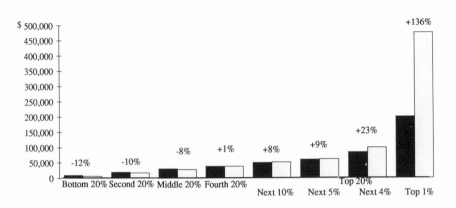

SOURCE: Congressional Budget Office data in, U.S. House of Representatives, Committee on Ways and Means, 1991 "Green Book" (May 7, 1991).

NOTE: Estimated 1992 dollars.

Finally, consider education (Figures 4.15 and 4.16). In a world where capital moves at electronic speeds and technology leaks very quickly, how does a nation stay rich and powerful if it grows dumber than its competitors? Note the performance of the Asian NICs, for these are no longer sources of cheap, unskilled labor. Their labor forces are in many ways more skilled than those in the U.S. and Europe, and their performance, in many high-tech areas superior to that of Europe, is directly related to their educational attainments.

The foregoing indicators, however imperfect they may be, add up to a troubled U.S. response to the challenges of the new international economy.

THE RESPONSE OF U.S. POLICYMAKERS?

The response of U.S. policymakers to this poor competitive performance by the American economy is difficult to explain, combining, as it does, equal parts of the Machiavellian and the Quixotic. A bold and determined economic policy has been consistently applied, but it is quite unclear what

Figure 4.15. Twelfth-grade achievement scores in advanced algebra for selected countries.

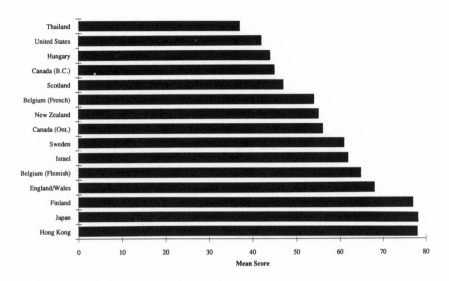

SOURCE: International Association for the Evaluation of Educational Achievement, *The Under-achieving Curriculum: Assessing U.S. School Mathematics from an International Perspective* (Champaign, Ill.: Stipes Publishing, 1987).

relation—if any—it has to the problems and context outlined here. It seems to be more a romantic reaction, a return to the simplicities and certainties of America's uplifting past—not as it was, but as it should have been—than a studied response to structural changes in the world economy. We can isolate three major themes of America's policy response.

(1) Deregulation and redistribution. With the fervor of a crusade, the government deregulated markets in such critical areas as telecommunications, air transport, and financial services (banking, brokering, etc.). After a dramatic start, the long-term negative effects soon began to be felt; and the severely weakened position of U.S. air carriers and banks is becoming better known every day.[10] There were also efforts to break unions, lower real wages, cut social expenditures, and redistribute income toward the

10. Telecommunications poses a more subtle set of questions. See Bar and Borrus, *Information Networks and Competitive Advantage*, BRIE/OECD Telecommunications Study, Paris, October 1989. Also see their *From Public Access to Private Connections: Network Policy and National Advantage*, BRIE Working Paper #38, 1987.

Figure 4.16. Standard test scores in mathematics and science for thirteen-year-olds in selected countries.

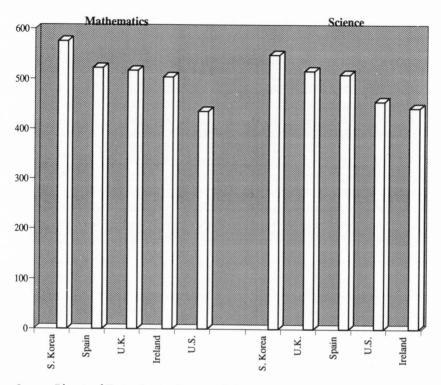

SOURCE: Educational Testing Service, Princeton, N.J., 1989.

NOTE: Scale = 0—1000.

top. Weak unions and lower real wages were supposed to make American enterprise more efficient and more dynamic; lower taxes, especially at the top, were supposed to spur initiative and to generate higher levels of savings and investment, thereby increasing competitiveness, the level of national income, and, as a second-order effect, government tax revenues without raising tax rates. As noted above, none of these final outcomes was achieved, although the intermediary objectives were successfully attained. Wages fell, inequality increased; but savings declined, investment stagnated, competitiveness weakened, and the government deficit soared. The government did not become smaller; it did not become less intrusive or more efficient. A newly invigorated automatic market economy did not sprout from the burnt forest of the mixed economy. The state did not wither away: it grew bigger and more intrusive, but ever less able either to act strategically and effectively or to achieve justice. Legitimacy declined along with efficiency.

(2) The second theme is an argument vigorously repeated by mainstream American economists which contends that America does not have a competitiveness problem; we have a macroeconomic problem, an imbalance of savings and spending that necessitates massive foreign borrowing and, therefore, by definition, results in large trade deficits. Cut the deficit (or, in its more sophisticated version, boost the savings rate) and the trade deficit will vanish. The real truth contained in this statement comes from the power of an identity.[11] It does not come from causal analysis. The identity also works in reverse: massive trade deficits necessitate foreign investment and borrowing as the dollars piling up abroad have nowhere else to go. Let us accept as given that the scale of the trade deficit is a macroeconomic phenomenon. On the policy level, nothing whatever has been done to change macroeconomic conditions. The government has refused to increase taxes and declared social security and defense spending to be inviolate. Interest payments, by definition, cannot be cut. That leaves less than 19 percent of total federal budget to absorb any contemplated cuts—not enough in its entirety to eliminate the deficit. This 19 percent includes such critical governmental activities as White House staff, U.S. trade negotiators, air controllers, and drug enforcement, not to mention various programs (with large constituencies) such as federal contributions to education, transportation, crime control, agriculture, water, welfare, etc. The policy approach has not been merely disingenuous, but irresponsible. The resolute inaction on the "macro" question did, however, achieve one important strategic goal: it prevented any new thoughts or any new policies. After insisting that all that was needed was a strong dose of traditional, unpleasant medicine, the government withheld the potion. Such fundamental new approaches as a strategic trade policy, an industrial policy, a technological development policy in an age of spin-on rather than spin-off (when civilian technology is ahead of military technology and dependency is reversed), or a manpower policy found no place in the higher councils of the administration.

Price sensitivity seems to play an unconventionally small role in the

11. $X + T = NFI = S - GD - I$, where NFI is net foreign investment, X is trade balance, T is services, interest, and transfers, S is savings, I is investment, and GD the government deficit.

U.S. trade deficit, and this, of course, limits the effectiveness of macro-economic policy. A currency devaluation, traditional theory holds, should certainly reduce a trade deficit if the devaluation is substantial and the new rate held for an extended period of time. But it didn't; at least not against Japan. Massive devaluation of the dollar against the yen did not significantly change the U.S.-Japan trade deficit. In 1985 the dollar hit a dizzying high of 245 yen to the dollar, and the United States ran a trade deficit with Japan of about $1 billion per week. By 1988 the dollar had fallen by almost 50 percent against the yen, to 125 yen per dollar, but the trade deficit had not budged: it still ran about $1 billion per week. (We might note that U.S. trade with Europe did respond to changes in exchange rates [see Figure 4.17], underscoring, in an empirical way, the new character of international trade and the importance of not relying on traditional analysis and traditional policy tools to conceive and implement strategy.) When, in 1990–91, the trade deficit with Japan finally did narrow significantly, recession in the United States was the major rea-son—along with a Japanese strategy of embodying generous dollops of Japanese value-added in the growing exports of the Asian NICs. This

Figure 4.17. U.S. trade balance with Europe and Japan, 1980–1990.

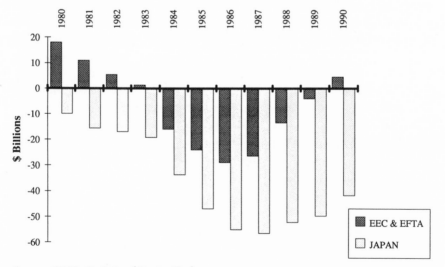

SOURCE: OECD, *Statistics of Foreign Trade.*

NOTE: EEC = European Economic Community; EFTA = European Free-Trade Association.

transferred to the NICSs, on paper at least, a segment of the U.S. deficit with Japan; but perhaps as much as 25–35 percent of U.S. imports from, say, Korea, consist of Japanese value-added.[12]

(3) The third major theme of U.S. policy is gaining currency in Europe—namely that what is happening in the U.S. and Europe is not so much an unwelcome but remediable deterioration of industrial activity as it is a movement toward a postindustrial economy of advanced services and high tech. President Reagan trumpeted this agreeable theme: "The move from an industrial society toward a 'post-industrial' service economy has been one of the greatest changes to affect the developed world since the Industrial Revolution. The progression of an economy such as America's from agriculture to manufacturing to services is a natural change."[13]

The New York Stock Exchange shared that view: it declared that "a strong manufacturing sector is not a requisite for a prosperous economy."[14] Segments of the business press expressed similar views. *Forbes* magazine was most graphic: "Instead of ringing in the decline of our economic power, a service-driven economy signals the most advanced stage of economic development. . . . Instead of following the Pied Piper of 'reindustrialization,' the U.S. should be concentrating its efforts on strengthening its services."[15] (In passing, we might note that America's strategy for the Uruguay round of GATT talks is predicated on this view that our future is in services and high tech and was built on a mid-1980s strategy of seeking through GATT a back-door approach to fostering deregulation abroad.) The problem with this commonly expressed view is that it is, quite simply, wrong. Worse, it is richly generative of disastrous policy.

Mastery and control of manufacturing is critical to a large, non-niche national economy. This fact, which should be central to policymaking, has been obscured by a popular myth that sees economic development as a process of sectoral succession: economies develop as they shift out of

12. Author's estimate. See also U.N., *Center on Transnational Corporations World Investment Report*, 1991, chapter 2 II, C.

13. Office of the U.S. Trade Representative, *Annual Report of the President of the United States on the Trade Agreements Program* (Washington, D.C.: GPO, 1984–85), p. 43.

14. New York Stock Exchange, *U.S. International Competitiveness: Perception and Reality* (New York: N.Y. Stock Exchange, August 1984), p. 32.

15. *Forbes*, April 11, 1983, pp. 146, 149. For a more academically respectable voice carrying the same message to a broad public, see Gary S. Becker, professor of economics and sociology at the University of Chicago, who writes: "Strong modern economies do not seem to require a dominant manufacturing sector" (*Business Week*, January 27, 1986, p. 12).

"sunset" industries into "sunrise" sectors. Thus agriculture is followed by industry which in turn is sloughed off to less-developed places as the economy moves on to services and high technology. Simply put, this is incorrect. It is incorrect as history, and it is incorrect as policy prescription. America did not shift out of agriculture or move it offshore, as the view from a window seat on any cross-country flight will show. We automated it; we shifted out of labor and substituted massive amounts of capital, technology, and education to increase output. Critically, many of the high-value-added service jobs that we were told would substitute for industrial activity are not substitutes; they are complements. Lose industry and you will lose, not develop, those service activities. For these service activities are tightly linked to production just as the crop duster (in employment statistics a service worker) is tightly linked to agriculture. If the farm moves offshore, so does the crop duster, and so too does the large-animal veterinarian. Similar sets of tight linkages—but at vastly greater scale—tie "service" jobs to mastery and control of production. Many high-value-added service activities are functional extensions of an ever more elaborate division of labor in production. Conventional statistics are blind to this relationship; so is input/output analysis. The shift we are experiencing is not from an industrial economy to a postindustrial economy, but rather to a new kind of industrial economy.

High Tech

The second axis of the postindustrial view focuses on high technology. It begins with a curious and ill-informed perception of high technology, which it sees as fundamentally a laboratory activity. In the United States policymakers discuss high tech as though it were properly undertaken by eccentrics in white coats at Berkeley or (for second-rate stuff) at MIT or Stanford. The entrepreneurial variation of this view sees weird youngsters renting Steve Jobs's garage in Silicon Valley to invent some improbable gadget. In all cases it is seen as an activity that is quite separated from the economy and, especially, divorced from production. Few views are quite so destructive to an advanced economy. Science—not advanced technology—is done that way; and it diffuses via its own channels, usually worldwide and instantly. Technology development is another story entirely: it is tightly tied to mastery and control of production, to such an extent that if you lose control of production, you will, in a few generations—and in electronics a generation is about two to three years—lose your technological lead. No ifs, ands, or buts.

A firm cannot control what it cannot produce competitively. There is little chance to compensate for production weakness by seeking an enduring technological advantage, for a production disadvantage can quickly erode a firm's technological advantage. Only by capturing the "rent" on an innovation through volume sales of a product can a company amortize its R&D costs and invest in R&D for the next-generation product. The feeble American presence in the current generation of consumer electronics is the cost of failing to produce competitively in the previous generation. Finally, if a firm simply tries to sell a laboratory product to someone else to produce, the value of the design is lower than that of a prototype; and prototypes are valued lower than products having established markets, as each step toward the market decreases uncertainty. A producer with a strong market position can often buy a portfolio of technologies at a low price and capture the technology rents through volume sales. For the firm, just as for the economy, manufacturing matters.

America's recent history in high technology has not been happy; in just a few short years we have lost our seemingly unchallengeable world leadership, and our position continues to decline. America still has the world's largest electronics industry, and in many segments the most advanced, but it is rapidly approaching number-two status. Europe's position is even worse.

Electronics

Let us survey in somewhat greater detail the most important of the high-tech sectors: electronics. Along with new (or advanced) materials and biotechnology, advanced electronics is at the top of every list of the industries of the future. But unlike other core technologies, advanced electronics is not just an industry of the future; it is already one of the biggest industries of today. Shipments by U.S. electronics producers passed $200 billion in 1987, about the same as for autos and about two and a half times the amount for aircraft (see Figure 4.18). And those shipments were growing by more than 10 percent annually. Electronics directly employs about 10 percent of the manufacturing work force, amounting to over 2 million U.S. workers. These data on the current size of the U.S. electronics industry do not include consumer electronics (televisions, VCRs, tape recorders, camcorders, disc players, phonographs,

Figure 4.18. The U.S. electronics sector (total electronics, 1988).

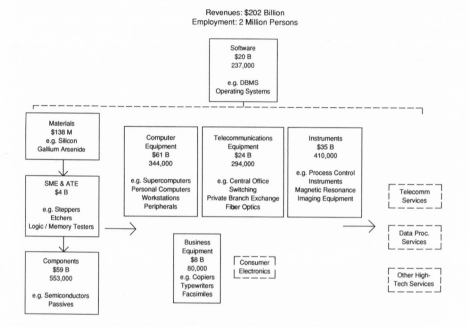

etc.) or the vast number of supporting jobs in other companies that do things for electronics companies, such as software programming, systems analysis, equipment repair, etc. Productivity gains in electronics run well ahead of the industrial average. Electronics is capital-intensive, exceeding all manufacturing by a wide margin. It is also research-intensive, spending more than any other industry on R&D (some 20 percent of all industry R&D spending); it is responsible for over one-third of all patents issued in the United States. Both the rate of R&D spending and its share of patents keep growing.[16] It is also an industry that is overwhelmingly located in the advanced nations, with over 90 percent of output located in the United States, Japan, Europe and Singapore, Taiwan and Korea (these NICs account for about 6 percent).[17] In this sense, electronics is not like shoes or textiles or steel or plastics or even autos.

Electronics has several distinguishing characteristics. The first is that

16. Data from U.S. Department of Commerce, *The Competitive State of the U.S. Electronics Sector* (Washington, D.C.: GPO, April 1990).

17. Ibid., table 8.

although it is a giant industry, like autos or chemicals, there is no such thing as un-advanced or traditional electronics, however national statistical offices and financial analysts may choose to slice up their categories. The technology simply moves too quickly. A five-year-old semiconductor is more like Ford's Model T than it is like a five-year-old car. A five-year-old camcorder suffers from surprising and unacceptable giantism. Like the digital technology inside the box that operates as either a one or a zero with nothing in between, electronics is either advanced or it is defunct.

A second characteristic is that there is a chain of dependency up and down the electronics sector. To put the question most simply, is it possible for an independent U.S. or European company to make a better computer and get it to market faster than Hitachi if it makes its computer with Hitachi semiconductors? Or, is it possible for a European chip maker to make a better semiconductor than Hitachi and get it to market faster than Hitachi if that semiconductor will be made on Hitachi chip-making equipment? The answer, for prudent policymakers, must be no. To complicate matters even further, the rate of technological change is such that one is quite ill-advised to take demarcations between segments (televisions, computers, telecommunications; systems and chips) very seriously. As electronics goes digital, these distinctions are likely to vanish overnight; companies or corporate groupings that are very strong in the core underlying technologies, as well as powerful, lean manufacturers, such as Matshusta or NEC, will quickly move into market niches occupied by companies that do not have a strong position (or a system of strong allies) in key underlying technologies such as semiconductors.

A third characteristic is that, to the extent such a thing exists, electronics is the classic strategic industry. It is characterized by large and important externalities, by rapid and multidirectional technological spin-offs, by formidable economies of scope, scale, and learning. Some of these can be captured simply by purchasing products and applying them well; many cannot.[18] European strategy in electronics will have to be guided by these three characteristics. Europe must be present in electronics in a big way; it must stay on the cutting edge of both technology and velocity production to get those products to market; and, most difficult, in order to do so it must reexamine the sector very carefully to decide what it must produce, what it can afford merely to purchase, and in what way it should arrange

---

18. See Laura D'Andrea Tyson, *Who's Bashing Whom?* (forthcoming, 1992; BRIE/Institute for International Economics, Berkeley and Washington, D.C., chapter 2) for the clearest exposition of what makes a sector "strategic."

its presence strategically. The most senior American policymakers, as well as the broad ranks of American economists, have been impressed by none of this strategic analysis.

America entered the 1980s with a strong technological lead and with a dominant market position in most segments of electronics. One exception was in consumer electronics (televisions, etc.), whose market was only about one-third the size of the market for computers. Consumer electronics was also growing more slowly than computers or semiconductors, and was assumed to count for much less in terms of technological sophistication. See Table 4.3.

Europe entered the 1980s with more size than strength in consumer electronics and found itself lagging further and further behind their best Japanese competitors (and increasingly exposed to new Korean competition). But Europe—unlike the United States—managed to hold on to its final market in consumer electronics (at least the television segment). It did, however, lose many of the newer markets. In recent years, European producers have made significant improvements in their television capabilities and have shown important strength in special applications, cleverly incorporating electronics into European-made production machinery, transportation equipment, and highly specialized equipment, as well as into various stages of the production process. Europe entered the 1980s with distinct weaknesses in semiconductors and computers. It enters the 1990s worse off in those key market segments and faces an immediate crisis: Europe's national champions—now promoted to European champions—teeter on the verge of either collapse in the face of accelerating international competition or complete technological dependence on foreign competitors. Increasingly, European producers suffer the worst form of dependency: they depend on components from firms that will also be their principal competitors in final systems.

Figures 4.19–4.21 and Tables 4.4 and 4.5 show world position in semiconductors. Along with America's declining share and the persistent failure of Europe to rally, there has been a striking shift in Korea's position vis-à-vis semiconductor production, coming from nowhere to challenge Europe (not just one European country) in total semiconductor production. Note also the data on semiconductor consumption, which may tell a more important story than production: Japan's share keeps rising; Europe's does not. Korea's semiconductor consumption rose even faster than its surge in production. Semiconductors, unlike beef or autos, are not consumed by individuals; they go into other products. Generally, if

Table 4.3. U.S. Share of World Electronics Market, 1984 and 1987

	% Share		
	1984	1987	$ Billions
Silicon wafers	85	22	>$.01
Automatic test equip.	75	68	1.2
Semiconductor mfg. equip.	62	57	6.5
Microlithography equip.	47	35	2.0
All semiconductors	54	41	$38.1
ASICs	60	50	7.3
DRAMs	20	8	3.4
Microprocessors	63	47	1.7
Computers	78	69	$121.0
Personal computers	75	64	47.2
Laptop computers	85	57	1.6
Supercomputers	96	77	1.1
Computer subsystems			
Displays	11	8	8.2
Flat panel displays	25	15	2.4
Floppy drives	35	2	2.5
Hard drives (up to 30 MB)	73	65	8.2
Hard drives (up to 40 MB)	70	60	2.3
Dot-matrix printers	10	8	4.8
Software	70	72	$44.5
Operating systems	90	90	16.4
Data base mgmt. systems	100	95	2.8
Spreadsheets	100	100	.9
Telecommunications equip.	33	32	$88.0
Central office switching	30	24	4.8
Fiber optics	75	50	3.0
Private branch exchange	29	26	7.8
Data PBXs	100	36	.2
Facsimile	30	25	3.1
Key telephone systems	28	22	5.7
Voice mail systems	100	100	.6
LANs	100	98	2.4
Data modems	49	37	3.2
Statistical multiplexors	94	35	.5
Instruments	52	46	$48.9
Medical equip.	35	41	12.3
Photocopiers	40	36	$13.4
Consumer electronics	19	12	$37.2

SOURCE: U.S. Department of Commerce, Science & Electronics.

NOTE: ASICs = application-specific integrated circuits; DRAMs = dynamic random-access memories; LANs = local-area networks.

Figure 4.19. World semiconductor production by global region, 1980–1988.

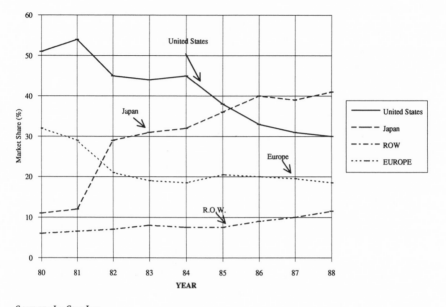

SOURCE: In-Stat Inc.

NOTE: R.O.W. = rest of world.

you are not putting many semiconductors into the product you make—and into the production system you use to make that product—you are making the wrong thing in the wrong way. Europe's relatively very low (and declining) position in the consumption of semiconductors is a most serious indicator of a troubled European position in electronics.

The future looks no brighter. Over the past three years national positions in emerging technologies (that is, technologies for which large markets do not currently exist but which will be of great economic importance very soon) have been examined in a series of independent studies. Each had a slightly different list of technologies, and there were several important differences in ranking; but overall the picture was quite consistent. One after another, the reports sounded alarms as they documented the erosion of America's position in advanced technologies and tried to alert American policymakers to the consequences.

The latest report from the U.S. Department of Commerce is represen-

Figure 4.20.   World semiconductor consumption by global region, 1980–1988.

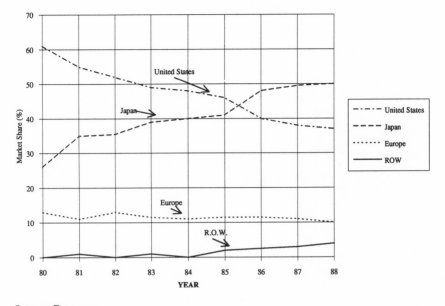

SOURCE: Dataquest.

NOTE: R.O.W. = rest of world.

tative. America, it finds, is not only losing its lead, but now trails behind Japan in advanced materials, advanced semiconductor devices and processes, digital imaging technology, high-density data storage and optoelectronics. The United States still leads Japan in artificial intelligence, biotechnology, flexible computer-integrated manufacturing, medical devices and diagnostics, and sensor technology. It is important to note that these reports place the U.S. behind Europe in only one of these technologies: digital imaging.[19]

The United States has not mounted an organized response to its threatened position in electronics. Europe has; but, clearly, the results are such that it will have to try something different very quickly. America simply abandoned the consumer electronics segment; recent talk about organizing a reentry strategy around flat panel displays and digital video

19. See Department of Commerce, Technology Administration, *Emerging Technologies* (Washington, D.C.: GPO, Spring 1990).

Figure 4.21.   Korea's position in world semiconductor production (total = $59.69 billion).

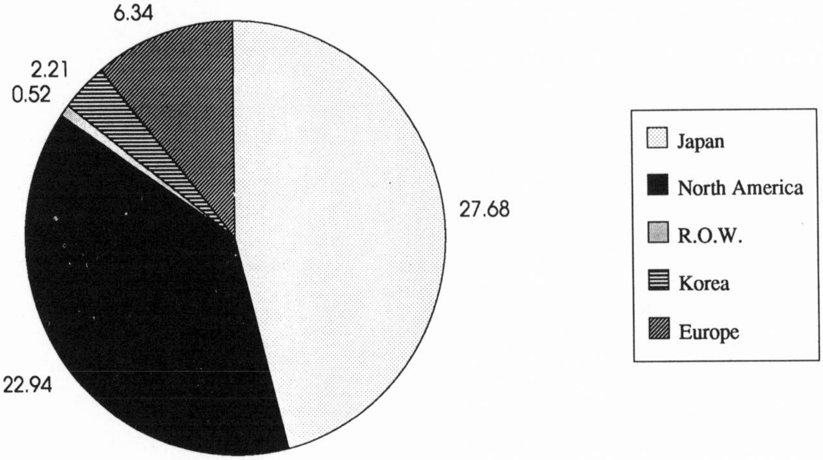

SOURCE: Dataquest, 1991.
NOTE: R.O.W. = rest of world.

Table 4.4.   World Semiconductor Production and Consumption, 1989 ($ Billions)

	Production	Consumption
United States	20.0	17.9
Japan	29.8	23.0
Europe	5.4	9.8
R.O.W. (includes Korea)	2.0	6.5
(Korea)	(1.8)	(2.0)

SOURCE: Dataquest.

has met with cold indifference, if not hostility, from the White House and a lukewarm response from industry. Only in conjunction with major foreign competitors (and there are only a few: Philips and Thomson from Europe or any of the big Japanese firms) will American players reenter that increasingly important market segment—and then only in a limited way, perhaps in signal processors or, one hopes, displays.

In the other major segments—semiconductors, semiconductor equipment, computers, displays, optoelectronics, etc.—America has refused to mount a strategic response to its eroding lead, despite a plethora of warnings from industry, blue ribbon commissions, the Pentagon, and informed observers of the sector. Some small and isolated efforts, such as Sematech and the U.S.-Japan semiconductor agreement, have received massive publicity. But in themselves, they are too small to matter and should not be taken as the tip of any American policy iceberg. This lack of a government-led response has become more important, given the existence of enormous government-led efforts in Europe, Japan, and Korea, and given the fact that the U.S. government's traditional method of intervention—the defense budget—no longer seems very effective in advanced electronics. Civilian technologies can no longer depend upon the military sector as a source of technology and early development. Indeed, the relationship has reversed: spin-off (using military technology in the civilian sector), which played such a powerful role in the infancy of semiconductors, computers, and jet aviation, to name a few, has, for the moment at least, ceded its place to spin-on, and the American military finds itself, like U.S. and European electronics firms, increasingly dependent upon Japanese civilian-based technology for its latest military technology.

The response of America's policymakers to the challenges of the new international competitive climate, in high-tech as well as traditional industry, has been ineffective at best, destructive at worst. What has been the European response?

EUROPE'S RESPONSE: SOME OBSERVATIONS

One could argue that the sudden acceleration in the movement for European unification—in shorthand, "Europe '92"—was, to an important extent, a response to the changes in international competition I have outlined here. After all, it is no secret that European industry would gain efficiency and power from a single giant market; but that was equally true and equally clear twenty years ago, or even fifty years ago, when Europe was worrying about its ability to compete with American mass manufacturers. And for more than five hundred years everyone has known that a unified Europe was a good idea, the only idea. Dante was perhaps the most eloquent exponent of European unification. The real question is not

Table 4.5. World Semiconductor Consumption Forecast 1984–1992 ($ Millions)

	1984	1985	1986	1987	1988	1989	1990	1991	1992
North America	6,020	3,692	3,799	4,913	7,295	7,997	8,000	9,550	12,006
Data processing	2,023	1,347	1,413	1,716	2,214	2,463	2,452	2,813	3,338
Communication	2,152	1,592	1,606	1,847	2,512	2,685	2,671	3,189	3,954
Industrial	970	699	724	844	941	1,057	1,029	1,166	1,367
Consumer	1,276	1,488	1,560	1,631	1,751	1,970	2,106	2,280	2,456
Military	698	788	848	918	987	1,052	1,195	1,372	1,664
Transportation	...	...	...	...	...	...	...	...	...
TOTAL	13,139	9,606	9,950	11,869	15,700	17,224	17,453	20,370	24,785
Japan	3,152	2,959	4,683	6,071	8,521	9,620	10,043	11,944	14,571
Data processing	1,025	985	1,454	1,949	2,772	3,039	3,037	3,659	4,602
Communication	822	758	977	1,157	1,691	1,875	1,818	2,169	2,766
Industrial	3,394	3,070	4,172	4,385	5,604	5,786	5,496	6,095	6,976
Consumer	0	0	0	0	0	0	0	0	0
Military	377	383	591	721	963	976	1,042	1,274	1,570
Transportation	...	...	...	...	...	...	...	...	...
TOTAL	8,770	8,155	11,877	14,283	19,551	21,296	21,436	25,141	30,485
Europe	1,010	1,380	1,583	1,851	3,265	2,977	3,023	3,455	4,791
Data processing	1,123	1,084	1,289	1,451	1,578	1,787	1,907	2,190	2,544
Communication	1,116	903	1,060	1,242	1,345	1,515	1,571	1,652	2,026
Industrial	898	763	843	889	944	1,037	1,116	1,606	2,144
Consumer	421	320	393	435	478	512	556	588	758
Military	237	271	365	487	591	667	756	979	1,215
Transportation	...	...	...	...	...	...	...	...	...
TOTAL	4,805	4,721	5,533	6,355	8,201	8,495	8,929	10,470	13,478

R.O.W.									
Data processing	⋯		866	1,480	2,372	2,682	2,744	3,380	4,153
Communication	⋯		284	471	752	937	1,175	1,524	2,057
Industrial	⋯		142	214	312	426	483	578	749
Consumer	⋯		945	1,542	2,409	2,888	3,138	3,917	5,088
Military	⋯		33	43	61	96	127	170	221
Transportation	⋯		95	144	208	249	265	318	397
TOTAL	⋯	0	2,365	3,894	6,114	7,278	7,932	9,887	12,665
Worldwide									
Data processing	10,182	8,031	10,931	14,315	21,453	23,276	23,810	28,329	35,521
Communication	4,132	3,621	4,620	5,714	7,525	8,226	8,571	10,186	12,541
Industrial	3,877	3,410	3,967	4,563	6,030	6,501	6,543	7,588	9,495
Consumer	5,262	4,532	6,684	7,660	9,898	10,768	10,779	12,784	15,575
Military	1,697	1,808	1,986	2,109	2,290	2,578	2,789	3,038	3,435
Transportation	1,312	1,442	1,899	2,270	2,749	2,944	3,258	3,943	4,846
TOTAL	26,462	22,844	30,087	36,631	49,945	54,293	55,750	65,868	81,413

SOURCE: Dataquest.

NOTE: R.O.W. = rest of world.

"Why Europe?" but, rather, "Why Europe Now?" To exaggerate more than just a bit, Europe '92 is a response to the rise of Japan. Of course, it is overwhelmingly a response to bigger, more complex, and more indigenous forces. Though today the movement for European integration is played out in the realms of high and broad-participation politics, it was a small elite in the mid-1980s that generated the sudden impetus toward unification. There is some truth, and much utility, in emphasizing the sudden impetus in the mid-1980s. It reflected the realization by critical segments of the big business and policy elites that the rise of Japan as an economic, financial, and technological power was effectively ending the postwar international order of a bipolar world. Europe's role in that world order was comfortable, albeit somewhat demeaning. It played second fiddle, depending upon and following American military, financial, economic, and technological leadership. Being second to the United States was one thing; being third, behind both the U.S. and a vigorous new Asian colossus of still-undefined configuration and intent, was something altogether different. Add to that the central meaning of this realignment of world power: a relative decline in American financial, economic, and technological power plus a complete eclipse of the Soviet Union. Europe's accustomed place—on the coattails of Uncle Sam—ceases to be quite so comfortable when the giant gives signs of weakening and wanting to sit down.

At the heart of Europe's response, and it is an epochal and wonderful response, is Europe '92. A few years ago, when the Europe '92 movement was first gathering steam, it resembled something like a Rorschach inkblot on which the Europeans had projected their hopes and the Americans (and Japanese) had projected their fears. Today, a better-informed reaction is becoming possible. The movement for European unification is a necessary response to the new competitive environment (as well as to other, more fundamental social and political factors). But as far as international competition goes, it is not sufficient. First of all, creating a bigger, more uniform market may well facilitate Japanese penetration owing to their decisive competitive advantage in such crucial industries as autos and electronics; Japan's entry strategy might aim at playing one government off against the other. Second, creating the giant single market for Europe's mass-production industries, and encouraging them to cooperate, consolidate, and invest more intensively in traditional mass production, will not change Europe's competitive position one bit; it may, indeed, exacerbate the problem. Finally, a simple Maginot line of protection—even at the new European scale—will not work.

In many ways, the new Europe is flirting with each of these responses simultaneously. For many good Europeans a single market means just that: open up the old continent to a mighty and invigorating blast of free-market competition from whatever direction the wind might blow. The invisible hand will then knock down generations of barriers to efficiency and, ultimately, arrange the pieces to Europe's advantage much more effectively than any imaginable (not to mention attainable) governmental guidance. In this view, Europe '92 represents not only a chance to remove the old structures of government intervention from the industrial arena but also an opportunity to dismantle the elaborate and costly European welfare state. The combination of a large and free market (with new economies gained from removing barriers and frictions and from increasing scale) and a reduction of the high costs of the welfare state would invigorate the economy and raise Europe's living standards and economic power. Seen from the considerable distance of California, the force of this European current seems much greater today than one would have predicted some years ago.

All this, of course, is a variant on the American experience. Yet no matter how the political dynamics play themselves out, in Europe as in the United States, not all protectionist barriers will fall. In the United States, in fact, new ones have been going up at a goodly rate. But one tenet of the American creed has been respected at all costs: protection has had no strategic function; it has been strictly a series of ad hoc responses to internal political pressure and, as a result, has generated little long-term benefit to compensate for its short-term costs.

There is, ultimately, no way Europe will remove all barriers to penetrating its market. If it did so, for example, in autos, there is a very good chance that the mass producers such as Renault, Peugeot, FIAT, and Volkswagen, as well as such speciality mass producers as Mercedes-Benz, would suffer fates as dire or worse than those experienced in the United States by GM, Ford, and Chrysler. So too would their respective regions and economies. The Japanese are perfectly able to demolish the European automakers. Their cars are cheaper and better. But political and economic pressures for a fully open European market may not be that strong. After all, who wants to open it? The Americans claim they do, but U.S.-European trade has not been a serious problem of balance for many, many years and will not become one. Except for a few small (albeit troubling) industrial subsectors, calm should be made to prevail. Reasonable diplomacy by European leaders should avert the worst international implications of a European market that is not fully open. U.S. automakers do not want to "open up Europe": they are there already, and have been for well over fifty years; they rightfully see themselves as good Europeans, threatened, like their colleagues, by major market openings. Indeed, they see themselves as perhaps the *most* threatened because no government will keep on supporting them. Perhaps most important, the German position ought to change soon. The Germans were all for free trade when they thought they could feed Renault and FIAT to the Japanese and remain safe at the high end of the market. But Toyota's mistake of going all-out, too soon, in the U.S. market with the Lexus—the "BMW/Benz" eater— is likely to swing Germany around to a more "reasonable," protectionist position, softer than that of Peugeot but real nonetheless.

Major U.S. electronics companies are also already well established in Europe, and for them a strong position in Europe is a matter of life or death. They face extinction if the Japanese push them out of the European electronics industry. Even the Japanese government talks of limiting Japan's share of the European auto sector, knowing full well that it will never be allowed to take the full share its competitive strength would now permit, and wisely seeking to avoid unseemly and uncontrollable crisis reactions by the Europeans—who are not likely to be so moderate in their response as the Americans. The tricky issues will not be at Europe's borders, except perhaps for one: exports from Japanese transplants in the United States, overwhelmingly autos, auto components, and electronics. Here there is much at risk for both Europe and the U.S. (and little risk for Japan). A clear and strict European determination of what is—and what is not—an American Honda or fax machine would be in the best interests of both countries. A major trade fight that sets the U.S. government as an agent of Japanese industry against the Europeans would be as unfortunate as it would be comic. While such possibilities exist, the diplomatic burden will rest primarily on European statesmanship.

Another major current, of course, is outright, full-blown protectionism with its usual rhetoric of job counts and "adjustment periods." But this view is credited more outside than inside Europe. Nonetheless, it is a view always able to find a real constituency. The serious vulnerabilities of key European industries reinforce this position and make it, ultimately, part of a final determination. That is to say, European protection will be maintained or enhanced in quite a few critical areas, including the two we have chosen to focus on.

Europe needs a strategic, competitive response at the European level. That response will rest on the scale and internal openness of the single market, but it will also entail substantial amounts of government action in order to protect and transform the structure of European industries in profound ways.

Europe will have to hold onto and strengthen its position in advanced electronics. To date, the first strategy has been the chosen approach: use the new scale of the European market to consolidate the old national champions into European champions. This strategy has not worked very well and is in imminent danger of collapse along with the industry. Bigness may well be an important attribute of successful electronics firms, but it is not the same thing as strength. Consolidations produce bigness but not necessarily strength: witness, in the United States, Unisys, the ailing consolidation of Burroughs and Sperry, a computer maker bigger than any European firm, and also a company not likely to survive much longer. GE and RCA, especially after their merger, provide another example of forging through consolidation an integrated electronics giant— one which then quickly exited both consumer electronics and semiconductors, deciding that it was unable to compete successfully against the Japanese. Neither scale nor a lack of integration was its problem.

In electronics, Europe has some difficult determinations to make—and quickly. It must hold the sector, but it cannot hold all of it by itself. So it must decide what is essential to produce and what can be safely purchased. The problem will be made more difficult by the recalcitrant fact that it will be much, much harder for the Europeans to sustain a cutting-edge presence in some segments than others—some of which are the most attractive. Whatever strategy—or strategies—are adopted, foreign-based companies and joint ventures with foreign-based companies will play essential roles.

Europe, for example, need not worry about a European presence in those advanced electronics products and technologies which are available from a great many companies in many countries. These are close to commodities in character. No policy, no strategy, is needed here. They should be purchased on the world market at the best prices and used by European companies in their final systems. Products made by just a few companies are more troubling, although they too may be prudently handled with the same sort of "buy" strategy. But products made by just a few companies, all of which are located in one foreign country, create much greater vulnerabilities. Products made by one or just a few companies all located in the same foreign country create fatal dependencies when those companies are direct competitors in the final systems in which those components are used.

The European computer industry is currently crumbling. The technological dependency of ICL on Fujitsu, for example, became so extreme over the last several years that there was no way it could introduce a next generation of product without de facto becoming simply a value-added distributor for Fujitsu—a relationship it has just formalized to the consternation of planners in Brussels. Bull too is technologically vulnerable. Likewise Nixdorf had to be absorbed by Siemens, which through huge effort and enormous cost seems to be holding on, while Olivetti and other European electronics firms are terribly dependent on the small group of Japanese companies for their core components and technologies—companies that are their chief competitors in final systems. The same is true for many successful U.S. computer and instrument companies: look inside Compaq's very successful laptop computer; there is very little Compaq present. Or try Apple's laser printer, or most anyone's for that matter. Advertising notwithstanding, no American company even makes a fax or a VCR, and they depend upon the Japanese for flat panel displays.

Willy-nilly there will be substantial direct investment in electronics in Europe by Japanese *keiretsu* companies. Europe should therefore require that they do R&D, product development, full production of the core components and next-generation product, as well as production in Europe. Europe must also organize to diffuse those technologies widely and quickly throughout the European production system.

A safer approach would be to pursue joint ventures with electronics companies that are not direct competitors with the European producers in their final systems markets. Today the American merchant semiconductor companies remain (outside the important memory segment) at the leading technological edge. Such companies as Texas Instruments, Motorola, Intel, AMD, National as well as many smaller outfits will not survive if they do not sustain their major shares of the European market. And if they do not survive, technological dependency upon the Japanese *keiretsu* companies will be nearly complete. That is the worst form of industrial foreign relations for Europe. There are natural alliances—in consumer electronics, computers, automobile electronics, "smart power," medical equipment, diagnostics, etc.—between American (even "outsider" Japanese) and European companies. They should be vigorously encouraged.

Eastern Europe

The second epochal (to use that big word again) element of Europe's response is not exactly a response—not something that Europe *did*, but rather something that has *happened* to Europe. Europe suddenly inherited a vast hinterland to the east and it must now decide what to do about it. Eastern (or perhaps Central) Europe poses a dizzying challenge. After all, it will be Western Europe that takes responsibility for aiding and steering development in those benighted lands, Western Europe that will bear the major risks if development fails there. This is a major challenge and, of course, a major opportunity. Eastern Europe has all those educated and dutiful workers that the Western European economies need. It is also a great new market that could provide years and years of respite from the international competition we have been discussing. If the world should split into regional trading blocs, Europe will be in the best neighborhood.

But Eastern Europe's vast reserves of cheap labor and untapped, unsophisticated demand offer Europe a dangerous temptation: to make the Oder-Neisse into the Rio Grande, leapfrog Portugal, Andalusia, and southern Italy and establish in the East, a step at a time, a vast network of cheap labor industrial plants under the control of European companies. Simultaneously one could import large amounts of cheap, docile, and easily assimilable labor from Eastern Europe into Western Europe's older industries and services, perhaps to replace recently imported labor that is proving difficult either to assimilate or ignore.

Before yielding to this temptation, Europe would do well to study the experience of the American economy over the last twenty years—an experience American businesses should profoundly regret. American companies, including good ones—once great ones—in electronics and autos as well as in lesser industries, moved production a stage at a time, starting with low-end, unskilled tasks and ending up now with very high-end, high-skilled tasks, to cheap labor reserves in the Pacific. There they availed themselves of labor that was cheaper and more dutiful (and, in short order, better educated) than what is now available in Eastern Europe. And they did so without waiting for massive infrastructural investments; infrastructure developed pari passu with the electronics industry. With great resourcefulness, RCA sought cheap labor and high-end niches as its primary response to early Japanese competition at the low end of consumer electronics. It got what it sought: good, cheap labor. It reinvested offshore, holding to its traditional approach to production, and lost everything to the Japanese, who were not allowed to go abroad for the cheapest labor and who, instead, managed to situate themselves on a new production trajectory. The Japanese path eventually led to absolute domination of the consumer electronics sector and substantial advantage in other segments such as semiconductors, displays, new consumer products, and, ultimately, computers. Today, in Eastern Europe, infrastructural needs are not so great; some cellular phones will do the communications job so you don't have to wait for state-of-the-art telecommunications systems. Moreover, Eastern Europe is nearby—not like the distant Pacific of the late 1960s and early 1970s.

For companies in the industries we are focusing on, autos and advanced electronics, the cheap labor strategy has not worked. For countries like the United States or the European nations, it cannot work. America's competitiveness problem outlined above, like Europe's, is not fundamentally with cheap labor countries. The trouble is with Japan, where wage costs no longer significantly differ from those in the United States or Europe. A low-wage European strategy to compete with high-wage Japan in autos or electronics is, on the very face of it, defeatist and will lead, as the U.S. effort has led, to defeat. After all, American producers fled to cheap wage locations and lost market share and technology leadership. The United States encouraged (or at least permitted) a vast immigration of cheap labor, and the Reagan administration tried (with somewhat less, but nonetheless real, success) to dismantle major portions of America's social support system. We even disinvested in the physical public infrastructure. America actually succeeded in lowering average wages over the past five years, and has kept them constant in real terms over almost twenty years. All in all, a political tour de force that Europe would be hard pressed—and ill-advised—to attempt. And it was all for naught. In the sectors we have focused on, the advantages from lower wages proved not to matter. Even an almost 50 percent drop in the dollar did not help. In other industries, such as apparel, the wage squeeze was simply not big enough, nor can it be.

Europe is and must remain a high-wage producer. It must increase, not diminish, its investments in education and radically improve the efficiency of those investments. In a world where capital moves at electronic speeds and technology leaks quickly, how can a nation stay rich and powerful if its people become dumber than those of other nations? America is not succeeding in answering that question, although it gives the impression of trying mightily. There is no answer other than the obvious: it cannot. Mass production once provided an out: it provided high-paying jobs to low-skilled, poorly educated people. But the emergent mode of production, flexible-volume production, offers no such protective shelter. It relies fundamentally on formal (not traditional craft) skills, on the ability to interpret symbolic data. That means first-rate, formal education.

Before Europe, in some futile quest for lower costs, sets out to dismantle its social protection system, it would be well advised to study the ironies of America's "cost savings" in such critical areas as child care, health, and social stability. These complement education and, like education and telecommunications, should be seen in the context of a realistic image of a modern production system. Under the old system, based on a massive accumulation of capital, a great many highly intelligent, well-educated people designed products and production systems in minute detail and many more uneducated and low-skilled people labored very productively to make masses of products which their high wages permitted them to consume. Production happened inside the plant and was, in the context of reasonable public order, controllable. But today a new image of the production process should guide social policymaking, one that sees production more as a network than a hierarchy, in which productivity is determined by the skills and attitudes of the person on the other end of the communication line. It is not easily contained within the plant, nor even within the firm, however big. If he (or she) is incompetent, so are you.

For reasons that elude reason, it seems very difficult for one great nation to learn from the mistakes of another. Europe has much to learn from America's experiences these past years. I hope it can do so without repeating them.

North-South Relations in the Present Context: A New Dependency?

*Si el viejo proyecto socialista de las izquierdas no da más
frutos, es que ha llegado ya la hora de construir uno
nuevo—uno que no solo viva de la protesta, sino uno
que esté animado por la utopia de un orden social más
justo.*

[If the old socialist project of the Left is no longer
bearing fruit, that is because the hour has arrived to
build a new one—one that does not live by protest alone,
but that may be animated by the utopia of a more just
social order.]

—Oskar Lafontaine

In the epigraph above, I quote a sentence from Lafontaine's article in the first issue of the magazine *El Socialismo del Futuro*.[1] That sentence summarizes the political challenge which the Left faces today.

Indeed, since the libertarian wave of May 1968 until the fall of the Berlin Wall, socialism and the Left in general have found themselves cornered, placed "in the spotlight" (*en el banquillo*). An entire tradition, which once blended reason and utopia, enlightenment and revolution, saw itself displaced by an uncertainty about the idea of progress and a disbelief in the dialectical "negation of the negation": as history unfolded, the victorious Revolution could no longer be seen.

On the contrary, the postindustrial world had occasioned a new libertarian wave, driven by a kind of "anguished pessimism" which in turn had been brought about by that existential anxiety over the real possibility of

1. Oskar Latontaine, "El socialismo y los nuevos movimientos sociales," *El Socialismo del Futuro* (Madrid), 1 (May 1990).

the end of the world (or, at least, of mankind) which nuclear terror and environmental destruction impose. To the ecological protest (which in many dimensions was antimodern, too, afraid of technical progress and incredulous about reasons of state, if not reason) was added an anti-institutional spirit, already evident in 1968 in the revolts on university campuses all over the world. From this political-emotional atmosphere arose the new intellectual currents: postmodernism; the fragmentation of knowledge (and of the world); distrust of the tradition of rationalism that had given birth both to liberalism and to the several versions of the socialist critique.

Certainly there were intellectual reactions. Indeed, the attempt to reevaluate the Frankfurt School (somewhat skeptical altogether and, in the version of the *Kultur Kritik*, full of antimodernism) undertaken by Jürgen Habermas,[2] as well as the revision of Talcott Parsons undertaken by Niklas Luhmann, were attempts to anchor critical thought onto the old pillars of reason.

However, the path the socialist movement is now trying to follow (whether "shining" or not, I don't know) did not originate therefrom. On the contrary, it originated in the shock that ensued when, at the last minute, the leadership of the Soviet Union under Gorbachev[3] recognized the enormity of the ecological challenge and the nuclear threat. It origi-nated, too, from the perception that although we are now experiencing the Third Industrial Revolution, and are now living in what Manuel Castells calls an "informational economy" (see Chapter 2, above), impor-tant areas of the world and segments of society continue to be downtrod-den.

That is to say, there is a *risk of barbarism*, both in the global dimension and in the societal dimension, and this risk will not be reduced either by a reliance on the inevitability of progress or by its denial through anti-institutional protest. It is this feeling of risk, of danger, of adventure, which, lacking the support of a belief in salvation (in revolution, in harmony, in certainty), makes any ideology (whether doctrine or "sci-ence") necessarily more humble, more "probabilistic," and less a well-spring of verities.

2. Habermas's first important book in this genre was *The Structural Transformation of the Public Sphere* (Cambridge, Mass.: MIT Press, 1989). See also *Knowledge and Human Interest* (Boston: Beacon Press, 1971) and *Legitimation Crisis* (Boston: Beacon Press, 1973).

3. Mikhail Gorbachev, *Perestroika: New Thinking for Our Country and the World* (New York: Harper & Row, 1987).

In this sense, the socialism of the future will have to adjust itself to a sort of "middle-range utopia," if I may put a new twist on Robert Merton's notion of "middle-range theories."[4] Nonetheless, Oskar Lafontaine's observation continues to hold: if socialism is incapable of offering hope, if it offers mere protest (ecological or anti-institutional), even if it is a "movement" and comprises other movements, it will still fail to pave the way for change that does not limit itself to mentalities and ideologies, but instead represents a political instrument for better days.

Accepting this weak version of utopia, we do well to accept the contemporary moment: that social justice and freedom are the pillars of the new socialism, that we all surrender ourselves to the supremacy of the market. But we must not accept its logic. The "invisible hand" (and even Karl Popper accepts this)[5] is not perfection; it exacerbates and accumulates injustices.

For hope to survive it is necessary to associate social justice and freedom with the political instrument. The latter will no longer be the union of state and party, even if both are reformed, for postindustrial societies (i.e., information economies) are "decentralized": politics is not the center of all change; nor do the state and the parties constitute the sole instruments for reforms. The "polyarchization" of contemporary societies, as Robert Dahl has pointed out,[6] is a fact. But, either we build *mechanisms* and *institutions* with which the citizen can relate, at various levels of society, to the *res publica* (the "public thing"), or the paths leading to the new society will not be established. We can and we must discuss the place of the "public," the limits that mass society and organizational society impose on the making of "public opinion." We can even dream of a rational public discourse *à la* Habermas or destroy the myth of the public man.[7] But we cannot escape redefining the scope of politics and extending it far beyond state and party.

Finally, in this brief introduction, which may not seem to address the theme proposed, but which, as we shall see, is necessary to clarify it, the

4. R. K. Merton, *Social Theory and Social Structure* (New York: The Free Press, 1949), esp. the introduction.

5. For example: Popper's lecture under the auspices of Bank Hofman, Zurich, June 9, 1988, published as "Algumas Observações sobre a Teoria e a Praxis do Estado Democrático," *Risco* (Spring 1990).

6. See R. Dahl, *Poliarchy: Participation and Opposition* (New Haven: Yale University Press, 1971) and his more recent *Democracy and Its Critics* (New Haven: Yale University Press, 1989), esp. pt. 5 ("The Limits and Possibilities of Democracy").

7. See Richard Sennett, *The Fall of Public Man* (New York: Alfred A. Knopf, 1977).

other pillar of socialism—the theory of exploitation (of classes and of nations)—has been shaken by an earthquake of magnitude 8 on the Richter scale: the technological-scientific revolution has greatly reduced the mass of the exploited who are necessary for the health of the capitalist system both at home and among nations. That said, what can be done?

THE PRESENT WORLD

It was Gorbachev who most vigorously helped turn the page of history, reducing Marxist salvationism to its present scale. But with what arguments? Basically by recognizing the two great elements that constitute the fabric of hope in the contemporary world: 1) that nuclear war no longer represents, à la Clausewitz, the continuation of politics by other means, but rather the extermination of mankind; and 2) that "centralism," of whatever stripe, undermines creativity and hinders technical progress.

The consequences become obvious. Security systems must be collective, driven not by fear of the threat one bloc may represent to the other, but by fear of the "end of the world." From there to giving preeminence to global issues and thus to ecology is but a small step. And, on the other dimension, when the idea of the centralizing state, of the global economic plan, and the rest is destroyed—to the benefit both of local decisionmaking and the democratization of society—one must then address the question of the market as an instrument for regulating the economy as well as the matter of political pluralism as an instrument for guaranteeing justice and legitimacy. Thus, one arrives at the question of setting up new institutions on different foundations.

There remains the issue of equality. It is obvious that although in the first moment, in the face of the "crisis of the empty shelves," even the issue of freedom yields to the issue of supply (as Boris Yeltsin noted recently) soon thereafter, the former Soviet society having been democratized, the issue of equality will reappear. It will reappear, though, not as an absolute value to be guaranteed by the revolution, by the party, and by the bureaucracy, but instead in relative terms of "more equality." No longer will the issue be one of "less state," as in the neoliberal wave (now perhaps in decline after Margaret Thatcher and Ronald Reagan), nor one of "more state," as in Stalinist Sovietism, but rather one of a "better state," aimed at correcting the inequalities caused by the market.

The welfare state once again? Why not? On condition that it be imbued with the signs of the present—that it be defined more as a "movement," creating new public spaces so that the citizen and the organizations of civil society may participate institutionally in social decisions, than as a collection of mere "social policies," supported by state bureaucracies animated by the doctrine of whatever party holds power.

In one way or another—notwithstanding the opinions of those social theorists who have seen in the modernization produced by capitalism the creation of "institutional orders" which were different from each other functionally (economy, culture, religion, society, technique, production, etc.) and which would interrelate in a rather hierarchical pattern under the state—a new model of social organization has surfaced. The new order is "decentralized," less functionally integrated, more "systemic." Decisions at all levels are adjusted by continuous feedback. Such a system adjusts to conflict and sets up an equilibrium between a desire for freedom and a fear of chaos (nuclear war, ecological disaster, etc.). And things can fall apart.

In regard to what we may call the "ethos" of this new world which has reached Soviet society, we may identify a strange victory of reason. When many thought that a postmodern era of total fragmentation was dawning—an era in which any sort of global view would be impossible, an era marked by the union of cybernetics and totalitarianism (the "brave new world" of 1984)—what happened was a strengthening of freedom, the pursuit of understanding, and a proliferation of global issues.

Thus, classes and nations in vast regions of the planet, although their differences have not been abolished, are experiencing a spirit of globalism and enlightenment. And all this is now being mistaken by many as a victory for competition, for self-reliant individualism, the market, neoliberal capitalism.

Sweet delusion or bitter disappointment? It is true that the Soviet world and Eastern Europe—even China—have returned to modernity in almost classical terms: market plus freedom. However, behind this marriage (which is not only one of convenience) there is a revolution in the mode of production and living that brings together humankind in a way that is very different from what one might imagine if one's explanatory framework were that of the "end of history" with the victory of neoliberalism.[8]

---

8. See Francis Fukuyama, "The End of History?" *The National Interest* 16 (Summer 1989).

The rationale that wins, as I said, is more humble and is hardened by the genuine risk of nuclear holocaust and chaos. The desired freedom is to be found neither in revolutionary salvation nor in the contest of private interests decided by the hidden god of the market. The new humanism, if I may say so, finds its proper subject more in humankind than in individuals and is therefore a collective humanism. And in the realm of practical action there is something new that rests neither on the individual nor on his soul, objectified in the state or in a bureaucracy, but on setting up "intermediary bodies," which are not, in fact, "bodies" but movements and new public spaces.

Behind these changes, I repeat, is the true revolution of our century: the marriage of science, technology, and freedom; of university, enterprise, and public authority. This "marriage" made it possible for the great technological revolutions (from nuclear energy and the laser beam, to biotechnology, to computers, microelectronics, and robotics) to go beyond the factory walls and affect the organization of society. This is why Castells describes the new global society as an "information" society and not merely postindustrial. The contemporary revolution reaches beyond the chain of production and kills "Fordism" and "Taylorism"; it revolutionizes the organization of the factory and of management; it reaches the public sector, the schools, the churches, the unions and, eventually, everything—not only through the new methods of management it permits, but also through the establishment of great mass-communication networks; not only through conventional electronic media (radio and television), but also through computer networks, facsimile machines, modems, and the rest.

All this, added to (and made possible by) the proliferation of the great manufacturing firms, the banks, the trading companies, and so on, provides the foundation for a globalized economy. And thus, along with the marriage of science, technology, and freedom, the great trend of the modern world is the globalization of the economy.

The centrally planned (socialist) economies collapsed because they were unable to absorb these changes and were unable to establish the necessary conditions for the evolution of this "new spirit." *Perestroika* ("restructuring"), along with *glasnost* ("openness" or "freedom") became necessary from the very moment when the USSR vilified cybernetics as a "bour-

---

Also see *La Fin de l'histoire et le dernier homme* (Paris: Flammarion, 1992), published in English as *The End of History and the Last Man* (New York: The Free Press, 1992).

geoise science." Thirty years would pass, however, before Gorbachev could openly criticize that attitude. The "organizational revolution," moreover, was never of any concern to the dogmatists of the "Grossplan." They still saw the world through infrastructural lenses. "Production" was their watchword, and productivity was to be improved only by investment in the "hard" industries—nothing "soft," no "human capital," no telemetrics for them.

The world of today, then, represents the victory of a "new rationality," of the technological revolution wedded to decentralized forms of management and decisionmaking. It favors a plurality of decision levels, making feasible a "polyarchical utopia."

AND THE SOUTH?

However, the Great Transformation—which caused centralizing authoritarianism to fall, which altered completely the forces of production and created the "information economy," giving new characteristics to classes and to class relations—*has not reached the whole of the planet.* Worse, while globalization of the economy caused the formation of new economic blocs, destroying the old East-West polarity and with it the U.S-Soviet hegemony, it also had a *negative and disintegrating effect on the Third World.*

In other words, the new "democratic-technological" revolution not only integrated the world economy, but it also paved the way for the emergence of larger and more powerful political and economic entities: the United States plus Canada plus (who knows?) Mexico; the European Economic Community; those parts of the East wanting to participate in the European experience; Japan and parts of Southeast Asia; and even incipient but promising agreements for the integration of the Southern Cone. At the same time, however, the old "Third World" fragmented along two or three main fault lines. What was once only a part of the Third World constitutes today a huge Fourth World of need, hunger and, above all, hopelessness. Other parts of the Third World managed to become part of the global economy: the old newly industrialized countries (mainly in Asia) and those countries which, though lacking a strong industrial base, have found niches in the world economy (e.g., Chile, the drug-producing countries such as Colombia, and, above all, the petroleum-producing countries). Finally, some countries of continental size—such as India, Brazil, and (to some extent) Indonesia as well as (with other characteristics) China—have been unable to make the entire integrating jump, but do have the necessary internal resources to escape the "quaternization" that leads to poverty without hope.

Therefore, we are no longer talking about the South that was on the periphery of the capitalist core and was tied to it in a classical relationship of dependence. Nor are we speaking of the phenomenon, described some twenty-five years ago by Enzo Faletto and myself in our book *Dependency and Development in Latin America*,[9] whereby multinational companies transfer parts of the productive system and the local producers are tied to foreign capital in the "dependent-associated" development model. We are dealing, in truth, with a crueler phenomenon: either the South (or a portion of it) enters the democratic-technological-scientific race, invests heavily in R&D, and endures the "information economy" metamorphosis, or it becomes unimportant, unexploited, and unexploitable.

So the South is in double jeopardy—seemingly able neither to integrate itself, pursuing its own best interests, nor to avoid "being integrated" as servants of the rich economies. Those countries (or parts thereof) which are unable to repeat the revolution of the contemporary world, and at the same time find a niche in the international market, will end up in the "worst of all possible worlds." They will not even be considered worth the trouble of exploitation; they will become inconsequential, of no interest to the developing globalized economy.

On the other hand, those Southern countries which do succeed in finding a way to join the contemporary revolution, even partially, will face still another problem. They must define how they will integrate themselves (i.e., a selective policy of "opening up markets," an appropriate industrial policy, an educational policy that makes it possible to integrate the masses into contemporary culture, a science and technology policy capable of supporting economic growth, etc.) without being swallowed up by the globalization of the world economy.

The problem is that the South's great comparative advantage, which once ensured its integration into the international market, albeit in a condition of dependency, has lost its importance. Basically, that advantage was an abundance of arable land, mineral resources, and cheap labor.

9. Fernando Henrique Cardoso and Enzo Faletto, *Dependency and Development in Latin America* (Berkeley and Los Angeles: University of California Press, 1979).

Thus, "quaternization" now seems to be the most likely outcome for those countries which can count only on such resources.

There has been, then, a *substantial change* in the dependency relationship between South and North and, I would say, it is a twofold change: 1) certain areas of the earth are of greatly diminished importance to the world economy (even considering their exploited and dependent condition); and 2) in other parts of the South, the challenge is no longer solely "economic" but now involves the whole of *society*. Let me clarify. In the past, it was possible to respond politically to the old dependency relations by appealing to "national autonomy," by demanding more industrial investment in order to correct deterioration in the terms of trade, and by expanding the domestic market in order to break the chain of "enclave dependency" and stimulate the internal distribution of revenue. Now the political response demands that the South, too, construct a new kind of society.

A future with dignity for the countries of the South will be achieved only with more education, a better state, enhanced productivity from its "human capital," and a great technological leap forward (information technology, new materials, environmental sense, and new modes of organization). Also required are a democratized society and state (necessary conditions, as noted above, for the marriage of production, university, and society in an atmosphere of freedom which is conducive to organizational and technological innovation).

A NEW DIALOGUE

So, we are back at the beginning. Paradoxically, in a world in which technique once seemed to generate the authoritarian control of everything, now this same technique presupposes freedom. In the advanced capitalist countries, as the failure of the socialist societies showed, without hope, without a utopia (even a "middle-range" utopia), there can be no continuation of "progress" (although progress is not inevitable, since both nuclear holocaust and error remain as possibilities).

In the Southern countries, priority must be given to societal reform. Otherwise, their positive integration into the world economy will not be possible. In this case, too, progress (hope, the welfare state, democratic socialism, social democracy) is neither the *necessary* consequence of the current challenge nor the only way to attain the democratization of society and state. But they remain as valid and contemporary options, provided they are brought properly up to date.

It should be noted that, in the face of the challenge of modernity and the impression that reason and the market are closely intertwined notions, the political concern in vast areas of the South is that the reaction against inequality can occur only through a strengthening of the national will perched upon the fortress of the state. Where this conviction finds the bases for its propagation in faith (as in Islam), cultural regression may be proudly presented as if it were an instrument of progress. In many areas of the South, discouragement seeks sublimation in new salvationist theses that substitute for blind faith in the inevitability of revolution (which was an attribute of the industrial world until the coming of the "information economy") through national unity against imperialism (or whatever epithet is now given to "advanced capitalism").

This regressive response, if not capable of shaking the foundations of the modern world (and it might well threaten them, as in the case of Iraq, forcing military reactions which are also irrational, even when aimed at wiping out evil) does absorb human energy. Indeed, this kind of response paralyzes vast sectors of the South, which, instead of seeking appropriate answers to their troubles (even more so in the Fourth World, which finds no answers at all), develop regressive ideologies. Skeptical about utopias, even those of "middle range," such movements create nothing but matrices for the local "counterculture," with only isolated repercussions in the hegemonic centers.

It is therefore necessary to redefine the dependency issue. This redefinition, however, so as not to yield only discouragement and a feeling that the South is either no longer of any importance or impossible to "integrate," will require a Copernican revolution of the kind proposed by Gorbachev. Just as the Berlin Wall did not begin to collapse until the moment when the former Soviet leader recognized the futility of war between the two superpower blocs and the impossibility of economic centralism beating capitalism, neither will the South—at least, those sectors where nothing but hopelessness is to be found—escape its perverse isolation until its problems are considered in a global context.

The "new humanism," the "global village," and "spaceship earth"—all these fine-sounding phrases become cynical slogans when they do not include poverty, backwardness, illiteracy, in short, the problems of the old Third World, as matters to be discussed and faced at a global level. This "globalization" of Third World problems cannot be approached as a unit, since, as we know, the South is not homogeneous. The term "new humanism" may mean, for many countries, something like: "renegotiation of the foreign debt in terms compatible with development, plus technology transfer, plus access to world markets." For other countries it may mean nothing less than the direct transfer of food, health care, and schooling.

What cannot happen is what has been happening until now: in discussions of the "crisis of socialism" and in reassessments of the effects of the "global economy," the South remains as a mere hindrance to which only lip service is paid. If the socialism of the future is to reclaim hope, it will be necessary to adopt a global approach and to treat as common issues, along with the environment, the problems of poverty and of rebuilding the *societies*, not just the *economies*, of the Third World. If this ethical dimension is lacking, the ideology now being prepared for a renewed social democracy will have the bitter taste of hypocrisy.

But it is not simply a matter of "ethics." Third World poverty, cultural regression in some areas, and the hopelessness all this brings will have an impact on the First World in various and menacing ways: migrations, disproportionate demographic growth among the "noninternationalizable" populations, terrorism, and authoritarian nation-states whose powers, though limited, can be menacing nonetheless.

Therefore, whether with a utopian vision or with a plan for preserving well-being already attained, the "new socialism"—or, more properly, social democracy—must address the North-South relationship in a new spirit. Just as there was a way to bring East and West together, there is now, in the new international order of the globalized economy, a gap to be bridged by a dialogue founded on realism and, at the same time, on solidarity, without which the populations of the Fourth World, at least, will continue to suffer in poverty and oblivion.

Epilogue:
The Resurgence of National Identity and National Interests

If the transformation of the technological basis of societies and the globalization of economic processes and strategies are the major trends dominating our rapidly changing world, national politics and culture are the prism through which these structural trends shape history. Nothing makes this clearer than the dramatic political events of 1992.

Bill Clinton's election signals the exhaustion of the laissez-faire economic model whose profoundly negative effects on American productivity and competitiveness we have documented and analyzed in this book. The crisis of the European Monetary System and grass-roots resistance to the Maastricht Treaty show the limits of technocratic political solutions to economic change. The chaotic disintegration of the Soviet Empire and the painful transition to a democratic, market society in the formerly communist countries of Central Europe are reminders that the path to a new order necessarily passes through a dangerous period of disorder. In short, new information technology and economic globalization have not only provoked structural shocks around the world but also reactions to it that are fundamentally political, and therefore different in each country.

Yet, despite these different reactions, the political debates underlying them revolve around common themes: international competition, regional integration, national identity, and national interests.

Just when global economics seem to dominate national policies and when information technologies give concrete meaning to the concept of the global village, the actual process of change to the new world order is itself increasingly dominated by nationalist interests. And the way these interests are manifested in politics and policies will ultimately shape the global economy, the informational society, and the new world order itself.

The Clinton administration seems headed toward a new form of state intervention in the economy. It is guided by strategic measures to enhance productivity, stimulate investment, and rebuild the country's infrastructure, and is best characterized as people-oriented supply-side economics. In this sense, the new economic policy is a response to the technological and human capital imperatives of the information economy. These are the kind of strategic government decisions that are vital in the new techno-economic paradigm—yet, traditional neoclassical economics insists on leaving them to the market.

The source of Clinton's electoral landslide was his program to revive the American economy, with emphasis on *American*. Putting people first and putting America first were clearly the key to the popular choice for Clinton, as they were the main source of support for Ross Perot's candidacy. The abstract arguments of free-traders and monetarists were overshadowed by the concrete realities for the majority of Americans of a declining standard of living and a deterioration of the nation's social and economic fabric. Thus, the defense of the national interest through an activist economic policy became the political response to economic globalization. With the fundamental threat to global peace eliminated by communism's collapse, the American public reinterpreted the national interest in terms closer to home, caring more about their economic welfare than their country's status as a superpower. Whatever the future decisions of the Clinton administration, its coming to power suggests that nationality matters in the management of both collective and individual interests in the new global economy.

The lack of attention by Eurocrats to the deep feelings of national identity and to the preservation of national interests has set back the process of European unification, slowing its pace and eventually threatening to derail it. Germany—the main continental player—is committed to unification despite its staggering social and economic cost. Such commitment has created inflationary pressures that have made the traditionally conservative Bundesbank even more cautious. Its tight monetary policy has forced all of Europe into an austerity program regardless of each economy's specific needs. Currency parity in the European Monetary System has become unfeasible. The lack of solidarity of the Bundesbank vis-à-vis the pound, the lira, and the peseta has shown concretely how the defense of German national interests contradicted the economic policies that other countries (particularly the United Kingdom) needed to reactivate their economies. This fundamental breakdown of European solidarity was further aggravated when France identified its national honor and political stability with the agricultural subsidies needed to maintain its low productivity and high-visibility farmers.

But the European malaise goes deeper. It lies in national identity itself. Faced simultaneously with supranational integration from above and ethnic diversity from below, Europeans are reacting with fear—fear of losing their identity, fear of seeing their national interests sacrificed to abstract powers of faceless bureaucracies and corporations, fear of losing political control of their democracies, and fear of being colonized by Japanese companies and invaded by Third World immigrants. These fears are translated into defensive popular votes against Europe on unification, as in Denmark; into a crisis of the major parties, as in Britain; or into the remaking of the political landscape, as in France. But fears have also raised the specter of Nazism, racism, anti-Semitism, and xenophobia—the old mechanism of finding scapegoats for the difficulties of historical transitions again plays into the hands of opportunistic demagogues.

Thus, the preservation of national identities and the positioning for the defense of national interests become critical ingredients in the construction of the new Europe. They force national governments to intervene actively in the global economy on behalf of their constituencies. Democracy has the fundamental virtue of connecting government to society, so that the rational blueprints issued by the experts have to be confronted with the expectations and reactions of the citizens to whom they are ultimately accountable. A somewhat unified Europe may still come into existence soon, but certainly not under the simplistic form of a Maastricht Treaty that has attempted to elevate statistical economic indicators to the category of international law.

The structural inability of nations to make the transition to the information age has also been a fundamental factor in the amazing disintegration of the Soviet Union and its satellite regimes. The strategy of looking for a rapid integration of postcommunist Central and Eastern Europe into the global market economy seemed to be the obvious way out of the historical impasse in which 400 million people still found themselves in the 1990s. The technological, institutional, cultural, and economic obstacles to the transition to a true market economy are formidable, and most of these societies, particularly in the former Soviet Union, will muddle their way through on a long and dangerous road. But the overarching issue commanding the entire process is the construction or reconstruction of national identity of each one of the new countries and of their states. The bloody convulsions in former Yugoslavia are the extreme expression of the historical tragedy being played out in Eastern Europe. Whereas the remarkably peaceful transition of Russia to postcommunism offers some hope for the future, such is not the case for other former Soviet republics. The whirlwind of demagogy and national radicalism may even push Russia itself onto a disastrous path in the coming years should the economic and political situation not stabilize. The future of Eastern Europe, and, to a large extent, of the entire world, will depend on the outcome of the process through which these new nations and their national interests are constituted in relation to the global economy.

As for the rest of the world, nationalism and nation-states continue to be the crucial elements in defining strategies in the global system. Japan's economic strategy is an extreme, though peaceful, form of fulfilling that nation's interests. China will become a world power on the basis of its dramatic economic growth resulting from its economic modernization and liberalization. And the various countries emerging from a disintegrating Third World also base their strategies on their national identities as expressed in forums such as the General Agreement on Tariffs and Trade (GATT), the United Nations Conference on Trade and Development (UNCTAD), and various regional economic and trade organizations.

The resurgence of national interests as the common ground on which to organize citizens, societies, and institutions in the global information economy forces theory to consider the interaction between the economy, technology, culture, and politics as the framework for understanding the new, emerging world. Instead of thinking global and acting local, as is often proposed by political activists, the political leaders of the 1990s will have to think local, relating to their own people, while acting global to reach out to the flows of power and wealth that form the structure of the international system. What has not changed in the global economy of the information age is that politics, not economics, is the stuff of which our dreams and our nightmares are made.

Index